CULTURES OF THE WORLD®

PUERTO RICO

Patricia Levy & Nazry Bahrawi

Marshall Cavendish Benchmark

NEW YORK

PICTURE CREDITS
Cover photo: © Corbis: Bob Krist
Giulio Andreini: 5, 8, 46, 49, 51 • Corbis Inc.: 1, 48, 112 • Sylvia Cordaiy: 30, 119 • Douglas
Donne Bryant Stock Photography: 3, 9, 12, 15, 23, 24, 28, 29, 44, 45, 55, 57, 58, 59, 63, 64, 66,
67, 68, 81, 96, 97, 98, 99, 101, 105, 110, 111, 115, 116, 117, 121, 122, 126 • Dave G. Houser/
Houserstock: 78 • Eye Ubiquitous/Hutchison: 38, 94 • Getty Images: 50, 104 • Getty Images/
National Geographic: 18 • The Image Bank: 42, 79 • International Photobank: 14, 21, 72, 78,
108 • James Davis Travel Photography: 6 • Björn Klingwall: 10, 31, 33, 40, 43 • Life File Photo
Library: 11, 34, 35, 83, 103, 109, 128, 129 • Lonely Planet Images: 52, 54, 86, 120 • David Simson:
4, 7, 17 (both), 56, 60, 61, 70, 73, 75, 76, 77, 80, 85, 88, 90, 91, 92, 93, 95, 106, 114, 118, 123, 124,
125 • Times Editions: 130, 131 • Travel Ink: 62

PRECEDING PAGE
Two young Puerto Rican women.

Marshall Cavendish Benchmark
99 White Plains Road
Tarrytown, NY 10591
Website: www.marshallcavendish.us

© Times Editions Private Limited 1995
© Marshall Cavendish International (Asia) Private Limited 2005
All rights reserved. First edition 1995. Second edition 2005.

® "Cultures of the World" is a registered trademark of Marshall Cavendish Corporation.

Originated and designed by Times Editions
An imprint of Marshall Cavendish International (Asia) Private Limited
A member of Times Publishing Limited

Library of Congress Cataloging-in-Publication Data
Levy, Patricia, 1951-
    Puerto Rico / by Patricia Levy. – 2nd ed.
        p. cm. – (Cultures of the world)
    Includes bibliographical references and index.
    Summary: "Explores the geography, history, government, economy, people,
        and culture of Puerto Rico" – Provided by publisher.
    ISBN 0-7614-1970-5
    1. Puerto Rico – Juvenile literature. I. Title. II. Series.
    F1958.3.L48 2005
    972.95 — dc22   2005009239

Printed in China

7 6 5 4 3 2 1

CONTENTS

A young Puerto Rican boy displays items of rock art for tourists.

**Strolling musicians
provide some street
entertainment.**

INTRODUCTION

THE ISLAND OF PUERTO RICO was for centuries the gateway to the Caribbean. Although Puerto Rico had few natural resources, it gave whoever governed the island access to and control of the region's fabulous wealth of silver, gold, and cash crops.

Puerto Rico expresses the spirit of its Indian, African, and Spanish heritage in its cultural traditions. As a part of the U.S. commonwealth, Puerto Ricans have permanently affected American culture with their vibrant lifestyle.

Puerto Rico stands at a crossroads, facing the decision of whether to merge its politics, economy, and culture with the United States or to become an independent nation and challenge its fragile economy to support its young society. There are small movements demanding autonomy, but many Puerto Ricans prefer to maintain the island's commonwealth status, and Puerto Rico's last two governors have opposed statehood.

GEOGRAPHY

THE ISLAND OF PUERTO RICO lies at the northeastern edge of the Caribbean Sea, 1,000 miles (1,609 km) southeast of Miami, Florida. Its closest neighbors are the Dominican Republic to the west and the Virgin Islands to the east. A rectangular-shaped island with a land area of 3,459 square miles (8,959 square km), Puerto Rico is about the same size as the state of Connecticut. The main island of Puerto Rico is 110 miles (177 km) long from east (Punta Puerca) to west (Punta Higüero) and 40 miles (64.4 km) wide from the town of Isabella in the north to Punta Colón in the south. There are also three offshore islands: Vieques and Culebra to the east and Mona to the west. North of Puerto Rico is the relatively cold Atlantic Ocean, and its eastern and southern shores are warmed by the Caribbean Sea.

A CHAIN OF ISLANDS

Puerto Rico is part of the Greater Antilles—a chain of islands in the Caribbean Sea that includes Cuba, Jamaica, and Hispaniola, which is shared by Haiti and the Dominican Republic. This region is also known as the West Indies. East of Puerto Rico, the Virgin Islands and another chain of smaller islands make up the Lesser Antilles.

A shallow shelf surrounds the island of Puerto Rico. Just 2 miles (3.2 km) off the northern shore, the sea floor plunges to 6,000 feet (1,828.8 m). The Puerto Rico Trench 75 miles (120.7 km) to the north falls even deeper—the 27,493-foot (8,380-m) Milwaukee Deep, part of the Puerto Rico Trench, is one of the world's deepest underwater chasms.

Opposite: **El Yunque National Forest in the Sierra de Luquillo.**

Below: **Puerto Rico has more than 300 miles (482.8 km) of coastline, washed by the rough Atlantic Ocean and the calm Caribbean Sea.**

The rocky coast at Cabo Rojo in the southwestern province of Pedernales. A lighthouse stands in the background.

REGIONS

For a small island, Puerto Rico has amazing geographical diversity. Its mountainous center is bounded by rolling foothills and flat plains. Rain forest covers large areas, and dry desert can be found in the south.

MOUNTAIN REGIONS The main mountain ranges are the Cordillera Central and the Sierra de Luquillo. The Cordillera Central stretches 50 miles (80.5 km) east (Manatí) to west (San Germán), with peaks more than 4,000 feet (1,219 m) high, including the highest in the country, Cerro de Punta, at 4,390 feet (1,338 m). A lower but better-known mountain is the 3,496-foot (1,066-m) El Yunque (The Anvil) in the Sierra de Luquillo. This area is a nature reserve. A smaller mountain range, the Sierra de Cayey, is on the southeastern end of the island.

COASTAL PLAINS The northern plain is a narrow strip of land 5 miles (8 km) wide and 100 miles (161 km) long. It is home to the bulk of the

population. The area was once fertile farming land where sugarcane and pineapple were grown. That has given way to urban and industrial development, with high-rise apartments, hotels, and factories.

The eastern plain is less populated but is a growing tourist area with good beaches. It had one of the world's largest naval bases, the Roosevelt Roads Naval Station, until it closed in late 2003, following years of protest by the local people. This area is a traditional tobacco growing area.

The western plain is still agricultural, with sugarcane, fruit, vegetable, and coffee plantations. Cattle ranches are common, and the area has been compared to the American West.

The southern plain is the newest tourist center. San Juan is one-and-a-half hours by highway from Ponce, Puerto Rico's second-largest city, which has been restored to its colonial grandeur. Some of this area is still agricultural land—the semiarid land is excellent for growing sugarcane. Inland from the south are the foothills of the Cordillera Central. This southern hill region grows coffee, corn, and beans.

A small town set in the foothills of the Cordillera Central. Most mountain areas are protected from exploitation, and many remain covered with primary forest, untouched by humans. The foothills have been cultivated for farmland.

Karst country. Surface water seeps into underground caves and tunnels, leaving unusual mounds, or mogotes, around 200 to 300 feet (61 to 91.4 m) high.

TURABO VALLEY Running west from the eastern coast into the central mountains is the Turabo Valley. It is formed by the meeting of three mountain ranges: the Sierra de Luquillo to the north and east, the Sierra de Cayey to the south, and the Cordillera Central to the west. Caguas, Puerto Rico's largest inland city, is located in the valley. The Río Grande de Loíza, the island's only navigable river, flows through the valley. This area is mainly agricultural. The town of Loíza sits at the northwestern end of the valley, separated from San Juan to the north by dense mangrove forests. It is home to many people of African descent who came here as slaves and then settled after slavery was abolished.

KARST COUNTRY In the northwest of the island in the Arecibo region is an unusual geological feature known as karst. One of the oldest rock formations in the world, a karst terrain is formed as rainfall gradually erodes limestone rocks along joints and cracks, leaving harder rock deposits. Since limestone is very soluble in rainwater, tunnels and caves form below the rocks over the years.

The karst region is also famous for the Arecibo Observatory, which houses the world's largest radio-telescope in a hollow basin formed by mogotes. Scientists from around the world use the observatory's state-of-the-art equipment to collect and analyze data on the earth's atmosphere and the solar system. For example, the telescope has collected data on Mercury, Venus, and Saturn, and it can detect asteroids.

OFFSHORE ISLANDS Puerto Rico's largest island is Vieques, 9 miles (14.5 km) east. A large part of its 51.5 square miles (133.4 square km) was used for U.S. naval training until 2003, when the facility was closed after massive protests by Puerto Ricans. Vieques has a small mountain range, some primary rain forest, and wildlife, including wild ponies descended from those bred by the Spanish settlers in the 16th century. The island's population is roughly 9,350, according to the 2000 census. Sugarcane is still grown on the island.

Farther east is the Culebra archipelago, which consists of a main island surrounded by 20 coral islets. The main island of Culebra is flatter than Vieques and has a few streams and a semiarid climate. According to the 2000 census, about 1,800 people live there. Most engage in subsistence agriculture. Many of the coral islets form a wildlife preserve for birds and turtles.

Mona Island, 50 miles (80.5 km) west of the mainland, has an area of 20 square miles (51.8 square km). It was once a lookout point for pirates but is now a wildlife sanctuary with a semiarid landscape. Mona is managed by Puerto Rico's Natural Resources Department and the U.S. National Park Service.

The islet of Caja de Muertos, meaning dead man's coffin, lies 13 miles (21 km) off the coast of Ponce. It is a nature reserve for endangered plants and animals typical of the dry subtropical climate. In summer the U.S. Fish and Wildlife Service closes many beaches on Caja de Muertos, because they are the nesting grounds of the endangered green sea turtle.

Puerto Rico's offshore islands attract tourists and nature lovers.

Although Puerto Rico is very mountainous, it has few large rivers because its landmass is so small.

CLIMATE

Puerto Rico is located in the tropical zone, but its high temperatures and humidity are moderated by trade winds, steady easterly winds that blow toward the equator. Temperatures range, on average, between 70°F and 80°F (21.1°C and 26.7°C), although some regions have more extreme temperatures. The weather is pleasant and cool in the mountains and on the coast, but it can get uncomfortably hot farther inland. In summer on the southern coast the temperature can go as high as 100°F (37.8°C), while in winter in the mountains it has fallen to 39°F (3.9°C). In the Cordillera Central the temperature drops one degree with every rise in altitude of 500 feet (152.4 m). December to March are the coolest months.

Rainfall is fairly even throughout the year, with a little more from May to September. Rainfall varies from 29 inches (73.7 cm) in the dry south to 108 inches (274.3 cm) in the mountains (180 inches [457.2 cm] around El Yunque). High rainfall often floods parts of Puerto Rico.

HURRICANE FORECASTING

The Caribbean has the world's third highest number of hurricanes per year. Forecasting when hurricanes will occur is extremely important. Through advance warning of impending hurricanes, people plot the storm's path on maps printed specially by local businesses. Puerto Ricans can also get regular updates about the climate from the National Weather Service Forecast Office in San Juan.

There is an interesting folk belief in Puerto Rico that when the avocado harvest is good, the country will be protected from hurricanes. This was put to the test in 1969 when Hurricane Camille threatened to hit the island. Avocado farmers assured the people that they would be safe because the avocados were good that year. Their confidence seemed to be well-placed, and the hurricane veered away at the last moment. However, many Puerto Ricans feel the need for added protection and keep a statue of the Virgin Mary and jars containing water blessed by a priest around the house for good luck.

June to December is a worrisome time for Puerto Ricans. This is the hurricane season. Puerto Rico has experienced 73 hurricanes ever since its first recorded hurricane in 1508. The most serious hurricanes hit Puerto Rico in 1928 and 1932, when many lives and millions of dollars in crops and property were lost. In 2004 Hurricane Jeanne left several people dead and caused floods, mudslides, power outages, and contaminated water supplies.

Although the Caribbean is in an active earthquake region, there have been no major quakes in Puerto Rico since the early 20th century.

RIVERS AND LAKES

Puerto Rico's strongest rivers flow from the Cordillera Central to the northern coast. The Río La Plata, the longest at 46 miles (74 km), has its source in the Sierra de Cayey. The Río Grande de Loíza, the widest, also has its source in the Sierra de Cayey and is the only navigable river in Puerto Rico. The spectacular Río Camuy Caves in the northwest were created by the Río Camuy, one of the world's largest underground rivers.

Puerto Rico has several man-made lakes formed by dams. These provide the power for hydroelectric plants, which once produced most of Puerto Rico's electricity. (Today the island's power is derived mostly from oil.) The lakes are mostly high in the mountains. Many are stocked with fish and are recreation areas.

MAJOR CITIES

As the population increases and more land is being developed for tourism, many smaller towns are beginning to link together into suburbs of the bigger cities. As Ponce and San Juan, Puerto Rico's two major cities, are only an hour's drive apart, some people live in one city and commute to the other.

SAN JUAN   Puerto Rico's oldest city, and its capital, was founded in 1521 by Spanish settlers. Its population in 2004 stood at approximately 1 million. Part of the city is built on an island linked to the northern coast

San Juan is a picturesque mixture of old and new, with classical Spanish architecture in the old parts of the city and modern steel and glass buildings in the business district of Santurce.

of Puerto Rico by a bridge. Its streets are iron-paved, its houses brightly painted.

San Juan is the industrial, economic, and intellectual heart of the island, with several universities, the main airport, and sugar, tobacco, and clothing industries. It is also a major tourist destination and banking center for many Caribbean countries.

PONCE With a population of 194,636 (according to the 2000 census), Ponce is Puerto Rico's second largest, as well as second-oldest, city. This major shipping port is located on the southern coast. It has an airfield, and a major highway links it to San Juan. Ponce's industries are canning, sugar, and iron. After a facelift that cost nearly half a billion dollars, Ponce is also a major tourist center because of its renovated historical buildings. Situated in a rain shadow, where afternoon storms are blocked by the Cordillera Central, it enjoys brilliant sunny weather most of the year. It is known to its residents as the pearl of the south.

MAYAGÜEZ The smallest of Puerto Rico's three major cities has a population of 104, 557 (according to the 2000 census). Its major industry, fish packing, provides over 60 percent of the tuna eaten in the United States. Many pharmaceutical industries are also located here, as is the University of Puerto Rico's agricultural college. The U.S. Department of Agriculture's Tropical Research Station, located here, has one of the world's largest collections of tropical and subtropical plants. Mayagüez is also home to Juan A. Rivero Zoo, the only zoo in Puerto Rico.

Fajardo is a sugarcane center and a port on the eastern coast. Boats leave from here to go to the islands of Vieques and Culebra.

15

FLORA AND FAUNA

A century ago, three-quarters of Puerto Rico was covered by forest. Today only 1 percent of its forests are original primary forests, untouched by humans. Puerto Rico's rain forests, semiarid deserts, and coral reefs contain an amazing diversity of plants and animals.

El Yunque National Forest in the Sierra de Luquillo has the largest expanse of forest in Puerto Rico. Part of the U.S. Forest Service system, and its only tropical rain forest, El Yunque has 240 species of trees, more than 200 types of ferns, and at least 60 species of birds. Puerto Rico's most famous animal is the *coquí* (koh-KEE), a small tree frog only 1.5 inches (3.8 cm) long whose sweet, musical call is often mistaken for a bird's. The Puerto Rican parrot is a rare creature. Only one flock of this endangered species remains.

El Yunque has a wide range of vegetation. Below 2,000 feet (610 m) grows the tabanuco forest. It is similar to rain forests in South and Central America and is named for a common native tree. Higher up is the palo colorado forest, a montane (high-altitude) forest, which is covered in mosses. Farther up, sierra palms provide tropical cover for steep slopes. At the very top is dwarf forest, stunted due to the thin soil on high peaks and ridges.

Elsewhere on the island, mangrove swamps, trees specially adapted to living in salty water, can be found. Their long, exposed roots provide a habitat for many animal species. On the northwestern coast is a subhumid forest, where satinwood and mahogany trees are becoming increasingly rare. (Mahogany plantations in Puerto Rico seek to preserve the species.)

The southern coast has a semiarid climate. Thorny, dry forest areas with cactus and spiny plants thrive there, as well as the Caribbean silk cotton tree, which can live for 300 years. Mona Island has vegetation typical of semiarid regions, including the tiny barrel cactus and organ pipe cactus similar to those found in the Arizona desert. It is also home to enormous lizards and iguanas and the booby, a red-footed bird.

The nearly extinct *ausubo* (ah-oo-SOO-boh), a kind of ironwood tree, is found in Puerto Rico. The wood resists rot and termites, and was used in many early buildings to make roof beams. When these older buildings are demolished, the Institute of Puerto Rican Culture salvages the beams and stores them for restoration projects.

Animals commonly found in Puerto Rico are iguanas, guinea pigs, and the mongoose. The most common bird is the *reinita* (ray-in-EET-ah), meaning little queen, which is very tame and often raids kitchens for morsels of food. Puerto Rico's many exotic species of arthropods include 15-inch-long (38-cm-long) centipedes with a painful bite. The poisonous black widow spider is also a resident as are several species of spiders that look dangerous but are harmless, such as the *araña boba* (ah-RAH-nyah BOH-bah), or silly spider, and the giant crab spider.

Along the coasts are beautiful coral reefs with fire corals and brain corals that provide a home for 2,000 different species of fish, including butterfly fish, red-striped grouper, striking orange and blue parrot fish, and pufferfish, which swell up when threatened. Jellyfish are also common around the coasts—Puerto Ricans call them *agua viva* (AH-goo-ah VEE-vah), or living water.

HISTORY

CENTURIES OF PUERTO RICO's past are tied to the history of colonial powers. The Spaniards colonized the island from the 15th to the 19th century, until ownership of the island was transferred to the United States. Since then, much of Puerto Rico's history has focused on its political status—whether it should become independent, remain part of the U.S. commonwealth, or become the 51st state of the union.

EARLY HISTORY

The earliest known inhabitants of Puerto Rico were the Ciboney, who migrated to the island on rafts from Florida via Cuba. They were hunter-gatherers, living on wild fruit, roots, and fish. Remains of their culture that have been found close to beaches suggest that they probably did not use iron or other metals. The Ciboney were followed by the Igneri, who came around 200 B.C. from Venezuela. These people also left traces of their culture through their multicolored pottery.

The Igneri were replaced around A.D. 1000 by the Taino Arawak, who called the island Boriquén, meaning Land of the Noble Lord. The Taino Arawak were skilled engineers and sailors who traded with other civilizations in South and Central America. They also farmed the land, growing cotton, corn, tobacco, cassava, and sweet potatoes. They ate poultry for meat and had no domesticated animals except dogs.

Although the Taino Arawak were peaceful, they were continually targeted by an aggressive neighbor, the Carib, who had nearly destroyed the Taino Arawak in the Lesser Antilles. By the end of the 15th century, the Carib threatened the Taino Arawak of Boriquén (Puerto Rico) as well. However, in 1493 Christopher Columbus reached the island, and the Spanish era began.

Opposite: **The fort of El Morro was built in the 16th and 17th centuries by the Spaniards to defend San Juan against attacks. Today the fort is a UNESCO World Heritage Site.**

THE SPANISH ARRIVAL

Columbus discovered Puerto Rico on his second voyage to the Caribbean in search of Hispaniola. He claimed the island for Spain, naming it San Juan Bautista in honor of the heir to the Spanish throne. But it was not until 1508 that the first Spanish settlers, led by Juan Ponce de León, established a settlement there. The Taino Arawak welcomed the settlers and helped them find a suitable spot to build a settlement. They called it Caparra. It was first situated on the northern shore of the island, but was moved in 1519 to the present location of San Juan.

After 1521 the island came to be known as Puerto Rico, or Rich Port, and its capital was called San Juan. The Spaniards' main interest in the island was gold. At first the Taino Arawak innocently exchanged gold jewelry for cheap trinkets offered by the Spaniards. When they realized that this was a poor exchange, they became reluctant to show the Spaniards where they got the gold or to help excavate it. The Spaniards then introduced a labor system called *repartimiento* (reh-part-im-YEN-toh) that forced the Taino Arawak to work for them in exchange for protection and for instruction in Christianity. It was like slavery, with the Taino Arawak forced to work in mines and on plantations owned by the Spaniards.

Eventually, the Taino Arawak were crushed by Spanish rule. Their religion was suppressed by Catholic priests accompanying the Spanish settlers, and they were forced to wear clothes for the first time. Many of them committed suicide and killed their children, believing that death was better than living in slavery. Many died from diseases that the Spaniards brought. The Taino Arawak rebelled in 1511, 1513, and 1518, but all were crushed by the Spaniards. Some Taino Arawak fled, joined the Carib, and began raiding coastal settlements in Puerto Rico. The raids and rebellions became so serious that a fortress was built in San Juan for protection.

In less than 100 years, Spanish rule in Puerto Rico completely wiped out the indigenous population. From 53,000 when Columbus arrived, the population shrank to a few thousand in the 1530s. In 1582 the governor reported to Spain that there were virtually no Taino Arawak left.

A PERIOD OF DECLINE

Puerto Rico was a profitable Spanish colony mining gold and producing cash crops until the 1530s when the gold mines were exhausted, the indigenous people were mostly gone, and the settlements were under attack by Taino Arawak and Carib raiders and French privateers. As Spanish settlers began abandoning the island, the governor banned all Spaniards from leaving. To set an example, he publicly cut off the legs of two men who tried to flee. To replace the diminishing population of Taino Arawak, African slaves were imported to do the manual labor. By 1530 half the population of 3,000 consisted of slaves.

By the 17th century Spanish power in the Caribbean had declined. The French, Dutch, and English gained more control and took over Jamaica and some of the Lesser Antilles. Puerto Rican landowners and ranchers were required to sell their goods only to Spain, but they began trading illegally with the enemies of Spain. An illegal trade in hides and sugar developed, particularly around Ponce on the southern coast. English, French, and Dutch traders openly traded goods, often with the Spanish officials who were supposed to keep these traders away.

The fortress of San Felipe del Morro (above) was built in 1539 to ward off attacks from enemies at sea. It was the strongest Spanish fortress in the Caribbean, with 18-foot-thick (5.5-m) walls rising 140 feet (42.7 m) above the sea. Another fort, San Cristóbal, was built between 1631 and 1771 to protect San Juan from land invasions.

GATEWAY TO THE INDIES

For centuries, Puerto Rico was the Spanish gateway to the West Indies, as trade winds blowing southwest guided sailing ships into the heart of the Caribbean.

In the 15th century Spain had control of large parts of the Caribbean and South America. As the British, Dutch, and French also began to establish a presence, Puerto Rico's strategic importance became evident. In the 16th century, Spanish fleets carrying valuable cargoes of Mexican and Peruvian silver were under constant attack by English and French privateers.

The French, English, and Dutch made many attempts to capture Puerto Rico in the 16th and 17th centuries. French privateers attacked the island in 1528 and 1538. In 1596 the first major English attempt to take the island was repelled. In another attempt, in 1599, the English fleet landed east of San Juan and attacked from inland, thus avoiding the strong fortifications built to repel invaders from the sea. San Juan was taken, but not for long. The Spaniards besieged the city from guerrilla positions inland and were able to drive the English out when the intruders were weakened by a dysentery epidemic. In 1625 the Dutch captured San Juan the same way, but before disease and starvation drove them out, they burned most of the city to the ground.

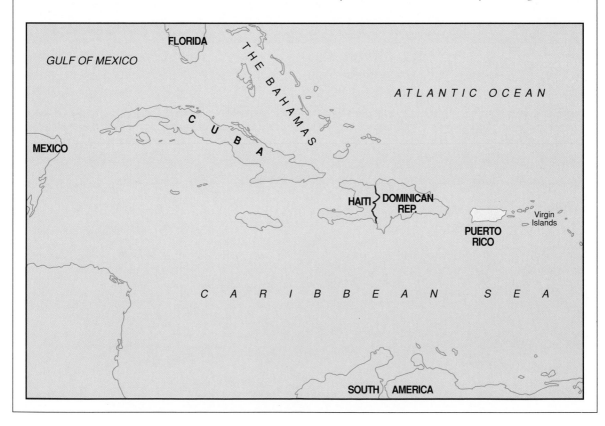

ECONOMIC RECOVERY

In 1765 Field Marshall Alejandro O'Reilly, an Irishman employed by the Spanish king, visited Puerto Rico to inspect the island and assess its fortifications. He was dismayed by what he found. The troops were ill-equipped, poorly paid, and undisciplined, while the fortifications were in a state of disrepair. Puerto Ricans were the poorest people in the Americas, and the island had no roads, few schools, and little sanitation. Illegal trade flourished with the English and French. The island's population was at a critical level, with only 44,000 people, including several hundred Spaniards and 5,000 slaves; the rest were racially mixed.

O'Reilly's recommendations to improve the island's defenses brought recovery to Puerto Rico. By the end of the 18th century, the population had tripled to 155,000, mostly as Spanish immigrants took up offers for free land. The increased population size made it profitable for ships to call at Puerto Rican ports. Military strength increased, and the island was better defended in 1797 when another English invasion was repelled.

Between 1750 and 1800, 18 new towns were established. Trade between Spain and its colonies was encouraged. Sugar, coffee, cotton, and tobacco plantations were improved with investment in machinery and with better trade agreements.

Sugarcane was brought to the Caribbean by Christopher Columbus in 1493 and was first planted in Puerto Rico in 1515. Puerto Rico's sugar industry received a major boost in 1789 when French plantation owners fleeing a slave revolt in Saint Domingue came to Puerto Rico and set up new plantations on the island. Since then, the sugar industry has been an important part of Puerto Rico's economy.

A mural in Christopher Columbus Park near the town of Aguada showing working conditions under slavery.

EARLY NATIONALISM

By the early 19th century, Spain's control over its colonies had weakened. There were rebellions in Mexico, Venezuela, Colombia, and other areas, until all that remained of the Spanish Empire was Puerto Rico and Cuba. This benefited Puerto Rico, which was once again able to trade with other countries in 1815. For the first time American trading ships became a common sight in Puerto Rican harbors. Puerto Rico traded sugar, molasses, rum, coffee, and tobacco for American wheat, pork, and manufactured goods.

By this time, most of the wealth lay in the hands of Spanish landowners and administrators whose loyalties were to Spain. Although most of the population were racially mixed peasant workers, there was also a Creole elite, racially mixed families who had developed a sense of national identity. These people began to demand partial independence, new roads, schools, and an assembly of their own. Spain replied with trade concessions, reformed taxes, and greater incentives for foreign settlers, but no political autonomy was allowed.

In 1868 growing nationalism, government repression, and the refusal of landowners to free their slaves erupted in open rebellion. Ramón Emeterio Betances, a doctor who became a nationalist spokesman, called for independence. He was exiled from Puerto Rico, and in 1862 he issued his *Ten Commandments of Freedom*, demanding the abolition of slavery, and independence for the island. From exile in Santo Domingo he began planning a revolution. Although Betances was captured, his supporters decided to go ahead with the rebellion.

AN END TO SLAVERY

By the mid-19th century, Puerto Rico's economy depended heavily on African slavery. Worried about the effect of slave rebellions in other parts of the Caribbean, the Puerto Rican authorities took steps to prevent this from happening on their island.

The Bando Negro decree of 1848 introduced the death penalty for any disobedient behavior by a slave, while any free African person showing resistance to a white man's wishes would have his right hand cut off. Just for being rude, a free African man could get five years in jail, and all African people from the Caribbean and the United States were banned from entering Puerto Rico. As a result of these cruel laws, many small rebellions took place and slaves ran away to the mountains.

In spite of pressure from other European countries, Spain kept delaying the abolition of slavery. Slavery was finally abolished in 1873. Even then, all slaves had to work for another three years and wait two years more before they gained full civil rights. When Puerto Rico's 30,000 slaves were finally set free, about half of them stayed as employees with the men who once had been their masters.

To deal with the dissatisfaction of the peasants and the middle-class Creoles, Governor Miguel de La Torre encouraged the islanders to have a good time. His administration became known as the regime of the three B's—botella (bot-ELL-yah), baile (BUY-leh), baraja (bah-RAH-hah), meaning drinking, dancing, gambling.

At midnight on September 23, 1868, Betances' supporters captured the town of Lares, arrested the mayor, and held a celebratory Mass in the town's church. They declared a republic, named a president, and offered freedom to all slaves who joined them. They moved on to San Sebastián but were driven back, and in the guerilla warfare that followed, most rebels were killed or taken prisoner. September 23 became known as Grito de Lares, the day on which independence was first declared in Puerto Rico.

By 1897 the nationalist movement in Puerto Rico had grown enough to force Spain to give Puerto Rico some autonomy. The 1897 Charter of Autonomy allowed Puerto Rico to send delegates to the Spanish legislature, elect a house of representatives, and take part in the administrative council. The governor was still appointed by Spain, although with fewer powers, and he nominated seven Senate members. In May 1898, after four centuries of Spanish rule, a new autonomous Puerto Rican government took office, led by Luis Muñoz Rivera.

THE SPANISH-AMERICAN WAR

On July 25, 1898, just a few weeks after Puerto Rico's new autonomous government took office, 16,000 U.S. troops led by General Nelson A. Miles invaded Puerto Rico and landed at Guánica Bay on the southern coast.

Although San Juan was bombed and there were minor battles with Spanish troops, the Spanish-American War was over in Puerto Rico in 17 days. Yauco was taken, Ponce surrendered, Mayagüez fell, and then the Spaniards surrendered. In December 1898, under the Treaty of Paris, Puerto Rico was handed over to the United States.

The locals were friendly. They knew the United States to be a rich, democratic nation and hoped for a better life under U.S. rule. The liberal leaders who won autonomy from Spain only to lose it to the United States demanded a referendum, but they were ignored.

LUIS MUÑOZ RIVERA

An important figure in Puerto Rico's history, Luis Muñoz Rivera is regarded by many Puerto Ricans as "the George Washington of Puerto Rico." He was a liberal-minded journalist during the time when Puerto Rico was trying to claim autonomy from Spain.

He played an important role in negotiating the Charter of Autonomy with Spain and was a key player in Puerto Rico's short-lived independence before the U.S. invasion in 1898. Under U.S. rule, he became Puerto Rico's representative in Washington, D.C. and successfully campaigned for the establishment of U.S. citizenship for Puerto Ricans, as well as an elected Puerto Rican legislature.

U.S. RULE

Puerto Rico's political status under U.S. rule was set out in the Foraker Act of 1900. Under this act, Puerto Ricans were neither U.S. citizens nor citizens of an independent nation. An assembly with a majority of Americans was set up. Its laws were subject to veto by the U.S. Congress. The governor was appointed by the United States, and Puerto Ricans ended up with even less control over their country than under autonomy from Spain.

Dislike of the Foraker Act grew so strong that the assembly refused to approve any legislation. The most important objection was the issue of citizenship. After many years of protest and negotiation, the Jones Act of 1917 finally gave U.S. citizenship to Puerto Ricans during World War I, when German warships were prowling around the Caribbean. Puerto Ricans could accept U.S. citizenship or refuse it, in which case they would lose many civil rights. As U.S. citizens, they could be drafted for military service and were still ruled by an American governor appointed by the U.S. president.

The 1930s were terrible years for Puerto Rico. Two hurricanes hit the island, and the economic depression brought mass unemployment and starvation. Conditions became worse than under the worst excesses of Spanish rule. The independence movement became more militant. Its leaders claimed that the United States' acquisition of the island was illegal since Puerto Rico had been an autonomous state at the time. Violence broke out in 1936 and 1937.

In 1943 the American governor of Puerto Rico, Rexford G. Tugwell, recommended that the U.S. Congress permit Puerto Ricans to elect their own governor. Finally, in 1946 President Harry Truman appointed Jesús T. Piñero as the first Puerto Rican governor of the island.

In 1898 the United States found Puerto Rico to be an island with 900,000 people—a tiny upper-class elite, a Creole middle class, and a vast majority of illiterate and poor, living in wooden huts and eating one meal a day. There were hardly any paved roads and little property of any great value.

THE COMMONWEALTH OF PUERTO RICO

In 1947 the U.S. Congress enacted a bill allowing an elected governor for Puerto Rico. In the first election for governor, held in 1948, Luis Muñoz Marín became the first elected Puerto Rican to hold this position. On October 30, 1950, the Puerto Rico Commonwealth Bill was signed by U.S. President Truman. Puerto Rico became a U.S. commonwealth with its own constitution. In June 1951, the people of Puerto Rico approved this arrangement and voted by nearly four to one to maintain the commonwealth relationship with the United States. However, the nationalist movement remained active and campaigned for complete independence.

In 1968 Luis A. Ferré was elected governor and promised a new life for Puerto Ricans. His reforms raised civil servants' salaries, cracked down on drug dealers, and set a minimum wage for farm workers. More importantly, Ferré set about improving the sugarcane industry with new technology and set up birth control clinics all over the island. Ferré's eventual aim was for Puerto Rico to become the 51st U.S. state, but this was opposed by those who favored the existing association with the United States and those who favored independence. In 1969 a crisis erupted after a Puerto Rican draftee refused to join the U.S. army. Riots between independence and commonwealth protesters followed, and 10,000 people marched in demonstration against the draft.

In the 1970s, political dispute over Puerto Rico's status calmed a little, although there were calls for another referendum to decide the issue. In the 1972 election, the governorship went to the pro-commonwealth party, and then in 1976 the pro-statehood party won control.

Through most of the 1980s and the early 1990s, Rafael Hernández Colón was governor. In 1992 he offered the nation a referendum on democratic rights that would have made possible an enhanced commonwealth status. The electorate rejected this. He chose to resign as governor, and Pedro Rosello was elected governor. His party favored statehood, so another referendum was planned, in 1993, this time putting the question of statehood directly to the electorate. Statehood lost, with 46.3 percent of the vote, to commonwealth, with 48.6 percent. In the next referendum, held in 1998, statehood lost again, with 46.5 percent of the vote, but this time to a different contender. "None of the above" won 50.3 percent of the vote. This figure included commonwealth supporters who rejected the referendum's definition of commonwealth.

In January 2005, Anibal Acevedo-Vila, a supporter of the island's commonwealth status, was elected governor, signaling the continued struggle of Puerto Ricans in favor of statehood or independence.

A labor protest in San Juan. About 11 percent of the workforce is unionized.

GOVERNMENT

PUERTO RICO'S POLITICAL STATUS changed in 1950. It ceased to be a U.S. protectorate or colony and became part of the U.S. commonwealth. Puerto Rico is a self-governing territory, although the United States has some control over its internal affairs. Puerto Rico's constitution is similar to that of the United States, with a democratically elected government consisting of executive, legislative, and judicial branches.

Some aspects of Puerto Rico's government are handled by the federal government of the United States. This includes all the island's foreign affairs and defense, internal matters such as the post office, customs, and quarantine, and other matters such as interstate trade, foreign relations and commerce, immigration and emigration, nationality and citizenship, currency, and communications.

Left: **La Fortaleza, built in 1533, was the first Spanish fortress to be built in Puerto Rico. It guarded the Bay of San Juan in the 16th century but is now the home of the governor of Puerto Rico. It is the oldest governor's mansion in use today in all the Americas.**

Opposite: **Built in the late 1920s, the Capitol Building in San Juan houses Puerto Rico's legislature.**

Although they are U.S. citizens, Puerto Ricans do not have the right to vote in U.S. presidential elections. Puerto Rico has one representative in the U.S. Congress, but this representative cannot vote on legislation before Congress. Puerto Ricans are eligible to serve in the U.S. armed forces and have fought for the United States in four wars.

The U.S. Federal Aviation Administration, Federal Communications Commission, Federal Housing Administration, and Federal Bureau of Investigation operate on the island. These agencies employ many Puerto Ricans, whose salaries are paid from Washington, D.C. In return, the United States receives benefits such as land for naval and military bases.

THE CONSTITUTION

The constitution of Puerto Rico prohibits the death penalty and phone tapping, and printing presses are safe from closure or confiscation by the state. Discrimination on the basis of race, color, sex, birth, social origins, or political or religious convictions is unconstitutional. The constitution guarantees the right to a minimum wage, an eight-hour work day, and special rates for overtime pay, as well as collective bargaining, unions, striking, and picketing.

THE EXECUTIVE

The governor is head of the executive branch and commander-in-chief of the National Guard, which is administered and funded by the U.S. government. He or she is elected every four years and must be Puerto Rican, at least 35 years old, a U.S. citizen, and a resident of the country.

With the consent of the legislature, the governor chooses the heads of the executive departments of justice, education, health, agriculture, commerce, finance, labor, public works, and state and social services. They are answerable only to the governor. Also reporting directly to the governor are executive agencies and public corporations, urban renewal organizations, the bus authority, and educational bodies such as the universities. The secretary of state succeeds the governor upon the latter's death, or removal from office.

THE LEGISLATURE

Puerto Rico has a bicameral legislature—a Senate and a House of Representatives. Twenty-seven members are elected to the Senate and 51 members to the House of Representatives. To prevent any one party from dominating the legislature, the number of seats is increased—the Senate now has 29—if one party wins two-thirds or more of the seats. The new seats are given to minority parties according to their support among the electorate.

Senators and representatives in Puerto Rico's legislature can be non-Puerto Ricans but must have lived in Puerto Rico for two years. They must be U.S. citizens, at least 30 years old, and be able to write either Spanish or English. When creating new laws, the legislature can overrule the governor's veto on a bill if it has been passed twice by a two-thirds majority. Most members have other occupations besides their responsibilities as legislators.

The Senate and House of Representatives meet at the Capitol Building in San Juan.

The Customs House by the San Juan harbor flies the U.S. and Puerto Rican flags. Customs matters in Puerto Rico are administered by the U.S. Customs Service.

THE JUDICIARY

Puerto Rico's judicial system is headed by its Supreme Court with seven judges. Below this is a Court of Appeals, a Court of First Instance, and a District Court. If a case is disputed in any of these courts, it goes to a higher court until it reaches the U.S. Supreme Court.

Puerto Rico's judges are appointed by the governor with the Senate's consent. They cannot take part in any political activity, and they have some independence from the executive and legislative branches.

Since 1950 there has been a great increase in crime in Puerto Rico, particularly in drug-related crimes, mugging, burglary, and homicide. The courts are faced with a large backlog of people awaiting trial. The constitution prohibits anyone being held in jail more than six months while waiting for trial.

POLITICAL PARTIES

Puerto Rico's political parties are split on the island's political status. The Popular Democratic Party (PPD) favors staying a U.S. commonwealth, while the New Progressive Party (PNP) supports becoming a U.S. state. These two parties have dominated Puerto Rican politics for 40 years, although the last two governors came from the PPD. Some other parties are the Puerto Rican Independence Party (PIP), which favors complete independence; the National Democratic Party of Puerto Rico, which is part of the U.S. Democratic Party; and the National Republican Party of Puerto Rico, which is part of the U.S. Republican Party.

Political banners outside the Capitol Building in San Juan.

COMMONWEALTH, UNION, OR INDEPENDENCE?

Discussion of Puerto Rico's political future is an emotional issue. It is so hotly debated that many cafés and shops put up notices asking customers not to "talk politics" on the premises.

Puerto Rico has yet to decide on its political status, an issue that has dominated the island's politics for more than 90 years, although it has become an issue more of economics than of governance.

Being a U.S. commonwealth has brought considerable revenue and foreign investment to Puerto Rico. But Puerto Rico lost its tax-break standing in 1996, so U.S. industry investors no longer enjoy the former economic advantages of doing business in Puerto Rico. This has created doubt on the benefits of the island's commonwealth status and sparked debate concerning independence. On the other hand, those advocating statehood say that joining the United States union would increase welfare money to the poor of the island.

Opponents to statehood argue that becoming a federal state means having to pay federal taxes, which would be a heavy burden for Puerto Ricans, who already pay high local taxes. Another argument is that the island would run the risk of becoming the union's poorest state and of losing its unique culture as it is absorbed into mainstream American life. Many Puerto Ricans would also find it unacceptable to lose Spanish as their national language and to adopt English.

Nevertheless, dissastisfaction with the current status is widespread. Pro-commonwealth leaders have proposed the establishment of an Associated Republic or Free Association similar to those in effect for Palau or the Marshall Islands, while left-wing PPD members have proposed a less conservative and more nationalistic stand.

With so many options, the issue has become very complicated. Whatever choice they make eventually, Puerto Ricans must address the fact that the island's close association with the United States has also led to its economic dependence on the United States.

LUIS MUÑOZ MARÍN

One of the most important leaders in Puerto Rico's modern political history was Luis Muñoz Marín, son of Luis Muñoz Rivera.

Born in Puerto Rico, Muñoz Marín was educated in the United States and spent some of his youth living in New York. In 1938 he returned to Puerto Rico and formed the Popular Democratic Party (PPD). He became a very popular figure as he traveled around the countryside drumming up support for the party, whose slogan was *Pan, Tierra, y Libertad* (Bread, Land, and Liberty). He was successful in gaining the support of the rural people.

Muñoz Marín won a seat in the Puerto Rican assembly in 1940 and became a dominant figure in Puerto Rican politics for the next 24 years. His policy was that the political status of Puerto Ricans did not matter; what mattered was their material well-being, and he set about improving that. He played a major part in Operation Bootstrap, which revitalized the economy and guided it away from agriculture and toward industry.

Muñoz Marín was also successful in persuading Washington to allow Puerto Rico some autonomy. As a result, a provisional Puerto Rican governor replaced the usual U.S. appointee in 1946, and in 1948 Muñoz Marín himself was elected governor.

Muñoz Marín remained governor until 1964, when he retired. However, he remained a strong political figure after retirement from public life. In 1966 he played a part in persuading President John F. Kennedy to appoint a commission to look into Puerto Rico's status. Muñoz Marín wanted to retain Puerto Rico's commonwealth status rather than join the union. In a plebiscite in 1967, two-thirds of the votes cast supported his call for remaining a commonwealth.

ECONOMY

PUERTO RICO is one of the most dynamic economies in the Caribbean region, with tourism being a major growth sector that accounts for some 6 percent of the gross national product. Manufacturing, once a major growth sector, was affected by the loss of the special tax-break status Puerto Rico previously enjoyed with the United States. Puerto Rico's per capita income of $8,509 per year is half that of the poorest U.S. state, Mississippi, yet one of the highest in Latin America. Puerto Ricans also enjoy one of the highest standards of living in the Caribbean.

Puerto Rico was historically an agricultural nation producing mainly tobacco, coffee, and sugarcane. Over the last 40 years, Puerto Rico has successfully diversified its economy to develop a flourishing industrial sector based on the manufacture of electronics and pharmaceuticals. This economic turnaround was brought about by Operation Bootstrap.

OPERATION BOOTSTRAP

In the mid-1940s, Operation Bootstrap was begun to revitalize the economy by building up an industrial sector in Puerto Rico. The government financed and set up factories to manufacture cement, shoes, glass, and processed fruit, among others. These became profitable by the end of the decade and were passed on to private developers.

In the 1950s the government began a massive campaign to attract U.S. firms to the island. The drive was so successful that by 1955 manufacturing overtook agriculture as the major income generator, with 500 factories employing 45,000 workers, all eager to improve their standard of living. In the 1960s U.S. petrochemical industries began to move to Puerto Rico. Some labor-intensive industries from the United States also relocated to Puerto Rico, where wages were lower.

Opposite: **A grass hat vendor in Puerto Rico.**

A booming manufacturing sector producing goods for export has made Puerto Rico an important port and shipment point in the Caribbean.

Puerto Rico enjoyed great social and economic progress in the 1950s and 1960s. Better wages and an improved standard of living quickly established a large middle class whose spending power attracted more U.S. industries. In the 1970s rising oil prices hit Puerto Rico. Economic growth slowed, construction halted, and many labor-intensive firms left for countries with lower minimum wages.

In 1976 another event reversed the trend and started Puerto Rico on its second phase of rapid expansion. Section 936 of the U.S. Internal Revenue Code granted tax exemptions to U.S. companies with investments in Puerto Rico, provided they paid 10 percent of their profits into the national development bank. In return, companies were allowed to keep 25 percent of their profits tax-free. New taxes were also levied on companies with investments in other Caribbean countries, to ensure that businesses did not shift out of Puerto Rico in search of cheaper labor markets. This made Puerto Rico a tax haven for U.S. businesses.

The new industries coming to the island were high-tech—chemicals, pharmaceuticals, and electronics. By the end of the 1970s more people were employed in capital-intensive, rather than labor-intensive, industries. By 1989 tax breaks were thought to account for 275,000 jobs, about one-third of Puerto Rico's total employment.

In a move to raise the minimum wage in the United States, U.S. president Bill Clinton terminated Section 936's tax-breaks for U.S. firms operating in Puerto Rico in 1996, thereby ending 20 years of federal incentives that had brought crucial U.S. investments to Puerto Rico. As a result, investments from stateside companies dwindled, creating an economic challenge for Puerto Rico's leaders.

MOVING BEYOND SECTION 936

When the U.S. Congress terminated Section 936 of the U.S. Internal Revenue Code, Puerto Rico lost the privileged economic position that had helped the island establish itself as one of the strongest economies in the West Indies. To help Puerto Rico recover from a dependence on the tax-credit benefits of Section 936, the U.S. Congress provided a transitional period during which U.S. companies that were already operating in Puerto Rico and claiming tax credits under Section 936 could continue to do so until the end of 2005.

In the meantime, the Puerto Rican government began looking for new ways to support the island's economy in the absence of Section 936's tax-credit benefits. Local tax incentives had to replace the incentives previously provided by the U.S. government. Puerto Rico's Tax Incentives Act of 1998 allow qualifying companies a maximum income tax rate of 7 percent, while certain industries, such as textiles and clothing, enjoy a special rate of 4 percent.

New tax incentives also favor European investors, giving EU companies preferential income tax rates for their operations in Puerto Rico and allowing them to repatriate the earnings of their subsidiaries in Puerto Rico. The island is promoting its location and infrastructure, and its educated, skilled workforce to attract investors from new regions and in high-tech industries.

A rum distillery in Puerto Rico.

PUERTO RICO'S WORKFORCE

Over the last 40 years, Puerto Rico's economy has changed from labor-intensive to capital-intensive. As a result, the workforce has changed from being a rural agricultural population with only a primary education, to a highly skilled labor pool. Over 20 percent of the population has a college education, and an even higher percentage is bilingual. Every high school graduate is guaranteed a job or job training, and the government offers incentives to firms to train their employees.

Employment figures are gradually improving. In the 1980s, the unemployment rate was around 20 percent, although this fell to 15 percent in the 1990s and 12.5 percent in 2004. The Puerto Rico Minimum Wage Law requires that workers not covered under the Fair Labor Standards Act (FLSA) be paid a minimum wage that is 70 percent of the prevailing minimum wage. There are different wage rates for different industries. Agricultural workers, for example, get a minimum wage of $1.17 per hour. Those who clock 200 hours or take home $200 for agricultural work are entitled to an annual bonus of more than $50, or 4 percent, up to a maximum of $80. About 11 percent of the population is unionized, mostly in the government sector and in tourism.

PHARMACEUTICALS AND ELECTRONICS

The United States is an enormous market for pharmaceuticals, and many U.S. companies have found it profitable to set up factories in Puerto Rico.

The island is one of the world's leading pharmaceutical manufacturers. In 2003 pharmaceuticals accounted for 66 percent of Puerto Rico's total exports and supplied 24.5 percent of world demand. Puerto Rico also has a strong electronics industry, particularly in computer parts. More than 17,000 people were employed in that sector in 2001.

U.S. companies in both these industries in Puerto Rico can take advantage of the Controlled Foreign Corporation (CFC) structure. They can sell their products to the United States duty-free and need not pay federal taxes on the profits made from these sales.

As Puerto Rico has no oil reserves, a nuclear power plant at Punta Hiquero generates electricity for Puerto Rico's industries and population.

Puerto Rican tobacco is used to make cigars. The main tobacco-growing region lies in the hills of eastern Puerto Rico.

AGRICULTURE

In 1940 agriculture accounted for 31 percent of Puerto Rico's net income, but its share of the island's economy has dwindled significantly since the industrialization drive known as Operation Bootstrap. The agricultural sector has also been plagued by problems of labor shortage and demands for alternative uses of the land. The chief agricultural products remain sugar, tobacco, and coffee, although dairy and other livestock products have replaced sugar as the primary agricultural income source. Other agricultural products include pineapple and coconut.

Sugarcane production in Puerto Rico reached a peak in the first half of the 20th century, as U.S. businesses brought machinery to make production more profitable. The rum industry, which grew out of sugar production, imports molasses, a sugar by-product, from countries with lower minimum wages. In 2004 more than 80 percent of the rum sold on the U.S. mainland was from Puerto Rico.

Coffee was the mainstay of the Puerto Rican economy in the 19th century but declined due to competition from U.S. coffee and damage to plants caused by hurricanes. Coffee is still grown in the southeast around Cayey and in the northwest around San Sebastián.

Coffee, tobacco, and sugarcane plantations all have labor problems. Since world cash crop prices keep agricultural wages low, many people prefer to live off welfare payments and food stamps instead of working on farms. As a result, there are not enough agricultural workers for these plantations. New programs have been introduced to allow low-paid workers to keep their welfare benefits while working.

A sugar mill. Sugar is made by boiling sugar-cane stems and pressing out the liquid. It is boiled again to form highly concentrated syrup and then spun in huge vats until it forms crystals. Before mechanization, the vats were spun by hand, but in modern refineries, the machines spin at 2,200 revolutions per minute.

With the decline of agriculture, food imports have risen a great deal. To reduce food imports, new ventures in farming have been started. The island has a team of agronomists who advise farmers on agricultural practices and suggest new ways of making profits. Farmers can rent government-owned machinery, warehouses, and packing plants as well as get low-interest loans to set up their own farms. A rice-growing program was set up in the 1970s—thousands of acres of land were flattened and a mill was built for the new industry, but the attempt was a failure.

Poultry breeding has been successful. Poultry is the fastest-growing farm sector in Puerto Rico, and the island is expected to become self-sufficient in egg production. Other successful projects are in cattle, fruit, and vegetable farming.

ENVIRONMENT

PUERTO RICANS became more environmentally conscious in the 1990s after several milestone crises. Perhaps the most important was in 1994 when an oil tanker ran aground less than a mile off the beaches of the capital, San Juan. The oil spill ruined popular tourist spots, such as Escambrón Beach, Condado Lagoon, and San Juan Bay. Realizing the dire effect of the oil spill on Puerto Rico's tourism-dependent economy, the government acted swiftly with the support of the United States to clear affected areas. The beaches of San Juan were declared safe within weeks.

Opposite: **La Coca Falls in El Yunque National Forest.**

Since that catastrophe, Puerto Ricans have shown active support for environmental conservation by participating in government programs and working with government agencies to protect the island's precious natural landscape and resources.

LAWS

Federal environmental laws that apply to Puerto Rico include the Clean Air Act (CAA), Clean Water Act (CWA), Resource Conservation and Recovery Act (RCRA), and Comprehensive Environmental Response, Compensation, and Liability Act (CERCLA). The CAA sets air quality standards that limit the level of lead, sulfur dioxide, carbon monoxide, and other pollutants in the air. The CWA prohibits the direct discharge of pollutants into waterways, and offenders are liable to criminal prosecution.

The EPA regulates the disposal of solid waste in Puerto Rico and aims to phase out land disposal of hazardous waste. The RCRA sets the framework for the management of land disposal of hazardous waste, primarily industrial waste. The CERCLA covers all forms of hazardous waste—on land, in the air, or in waterways—and manages the proper disposal of such waste as well as compensates parties for costs incurred in cleanup operations.

The more-than-10,000-hectare Luquillo Experimental Forest in eastern Puerto Rico consists of different forest types. Most of this protected area is primary forest, and there are areas for scientific research.

AGENCIES

Environmental protection in Puerto Rico is founded on the Public Policy Environmental Act of 1970. The commonwealth's Environmental Quality Board (EQB) sets out regulations and guidelines for preserving the island's natural ecosystems, reports to the U.S. Environmental Protection Agency (EPA), and must comply with federal requirements.

The EPA maintains an active presence in Puerto Rico through the Caribbean Environmental Protection Division (CEPD), which is based in San Juan. The EPA's Regional Disaster Response Team deploys staff to the Caribbean when hurricanes or other natural disasters occur.

WATER SUPPLY

After a drought in 1994 severely affected the northern part of the island, especially around San Juan, the Puerto Rico Aqueduct and Sewer Authority (PRASA) decided to build a super-aqueduct to improve the water supply to the northern municipalities. The route of the super-aqueduct, with its pump stations and storage tanks, was carefully planned to reduce its impact on the environment and archaeological sites. Completed in 2000, the super-aqueduct is fed by a plant in Arecibo that treats water drawn from two of the island's eight major reservoirs—Caonillas and Dos Bocas.

PRASA serves most of the island's population; fewer than 10 percent of Puerto Ricans, mostly living in rural areas, receive their water supply from non-PRASA systems. These do not always comply with minimum standards for safe drinking water. The Partnership for Pure Water (PPW), established in 1992, provides independent operators with training and funds to repair and upgrade their water systems.

Guesthouses and inns at the fishing village of La Parguera in the town of Lajas offer accommodation to visitors who want to picnic, see the phosphorescent bay by night, take a cruise on a yacht, or scuba dive. Such activities have to be moderated in order to control pollution to the country's waterways.

HURRICANE DEFENSE

Hurricanes are frequent in Puerto Rico; recent examples include Hugo (1989), Hortense (1996), and Georges (1998). Hurricanes cause death, destruction of property, and damage to the environment. They can cause water contamination when they damage waste treatment plants, and they leave debris in their wake, adding to the problem of waste disposal.

The government at the local level helps Puerto Ricans recover from hurricanes by making hurricane damage losses tax-deductible, and home mortgages require insurance for protection against structural damage caused by hurricanes. The federal government provides long-term technical and financial aid. Risk-reduction measures are part of the repair and rebuilding after a hurricane, making vulnerable communities more ready and resistant and reducing the future social and economic costs of hurricanes.

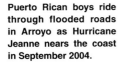

Puerto Rican boys ride through flooded roads in Arroyo as Hurricane Jeanne nears the coast in September 2004.

WASTE DISPOSAL

Dumpsites are a serious environmental and health concern in Puerto Rico. In 2004 there were 17 EPA-identified National Priority List (NPL) sites on the island. Such sites are reported to have released, or to pose a threat of releasing, hazardous substances that are likely to affect the physical surroundings or residents in the area. The sites include landfills in the Juncos, Florida, and Vega Baja municipalities.

Alternative waste-disposal methods include recycling, and converting waste to energy. San Juan and Arecibo, the regions that generate the most waste, have plants that break down waste to produce electricity, and Caguas will have the first non-incineration waste-to-energy power plant by 2007. Some municipalities encourage their residents to recycle, and cleanup campaigns attract active public participation.

Seabirds perched on poles stuck in the sand make a pretty picture at Luquillo Beach. Scenes such as this depend on the proper management of domestic and industrial waste.

PUBLIC AWARENESS AND ACTION

Developing public awareness of environmental issues is the long-term goal of any government's program to protect and conserve the natural environment. The government of Puerto Rico has, within the federal framework, vigorously promoted environmental education and given awards and grants for environmental efforts.

The EPA presents Environmental Quality Awards every year to individuals and organizations that make significant contributions to improving the environment and increasing public awareness and participation. In 2004 nine awards went to Puerto Rico in recognition of the efforts of

Puerto Ricans camp on the island of Vieques in protest against U.S. naval activity on the island.

two universities, a golf resort, a fishing and boating publication, and a pharmaceuticals company, among others.

The President's Environmental Youth Award (PEYA) promotes environmental activism among children and teenagers. In 2003 Puerto Rican Samuel I. Alejandro Rivera received this award for photographs he had taken of garbage-laden rivers. His photographs helped the community lobby for funds to clean up the rivers.

THE VIEQUES CONTROVERSY

Controversy has plagued environmental issues concerning Vieques Island, off the southeastern coast of the main island of Puerto Rico. During the 1940s the U.S. Navy incorporated Vieques, including the surrounding waters, into its Atlantic Fleet Weapons Training Area (AFWTA).

The closure of the naval station in 2003 cost Puerto Rico thousands of jobs and hundreds of millions of dollars in annual income, but the longer-term issue was the environmental damage allegedly caused by decades of military training, including live firing and weapons handling. This may have corrupted the island's ecological system with dangerous substances, possibly mercury, lead, napalm, and depleted uranium, which could pose a serious threat to the health of residents and tourists. Vieques is the most developed of Puerto Rico's offshore islands and is a popular tourist destination.

The U.S. Fish and Wildlife Service converted part of the former naval training area into the Vieques National Wildlife Refuge in 2001. The area's beaches, coral reefs, mangroves, and forests are home to several endangered plants and animals, such as sea turtles. In 2005, after much petitioning by the Puerto Rican government and by environmental activists, the EPA put Vieques on the National Priority List. The U.S. Navy is working with the government to confirm the environmental damage and health threat in the Vieques municipality and determine the necessary cleanup measures.

PUERTO RICANS

PUERTO RICANS CAN TRACE their origins to many parts of the world, including Spain and Africa. Puerto Rico's ethnic mix is visible in the different facial features and the range of skin tones among people who have lived there for generations.

Puerto Ricans have a few terms describing different ethnic types. The majority of the population has light brown skin and is known as *trigueño* (trih-GEN-yoh). People with Indian (Taino Arawak) facial features are known as *indio* (IN-dee-oh); people who look mostly Caucasian are known as *blanco* (BLAHN-coh); while people with very dark skin are known as *de color* (deh cohl-OR). Offence is neither meant nor taken by the use of these terms. The word *negro* (NEHG-roh) means dear one and is used regardless of appearance.

Left: **About 75 percent of Puerto Rico's population is *trigueño*—of mixed European and Indian ancestry.**

Opposite: **A family in San Juan, Puerto Rico.**

Puerto Rico has a youthful population. About half of its population is under the age of 22.

A MELTING POT

Evidence of the Taino Arawak heritage in Puerto Rico can still be seen in the high cheekbones and tawny-colored skin of some of the island's inhabitants. The racially mixed majority of Puerto Ricans have some Taino Arawak and some African features, from the slaves whom the early Spaniards took as wives.

Later Europeans who settled and intermarried in Puerto Rico included Scottish and Irish farmers in the 18th and 19th centuries. French immigrants came from Haiti after the Spanish Empire began to collapse and from Louisiana after France sold Louisiana to the United States in 1803.

South Americans came in the 19th century fleeing revolutions, and immigrant workers came from Galicia and the Canary Islands when slavery was abolished. In the 1840s, a labor shortage in Puerto Rico brought an influx of Chinese, Italian, Corsican, and Lebanese immigrants. A large community of North Americans settled in Puerto Rico before the Spanish-American War of 1898.

The 20th century saw yet more migrants fleeing to Puerto Rico to find refuge from political turmoil in their homelands. The Cuban Revolution of 1959, which started Fidel Castro's communist government, brought many wealthy Cubans from middle-class professions or those who owned their own businesses, while civil war in the Dominican Republic in the 1960s brought a wave of poor refugees to Puerto Rico.

Most of the inhabitants of Puerto Rico today live in dense settlements, especially in cities in the San Juan, Bayamón, and Carolina areas. Some 2 million Puerto Ricans live in the United States, and many alternate between the island and the United States.

THE TAINO ARAWAK

Although the Taino Arawak were completely wiped out by the Spaniards, evidence of their culture and lifestyle still remains. The Taino Arawak were a peaceful farming people who lived in villages, or *yucayeques* (you-kah-YEH-kess), of around 400 residents each. The villages had large houses built from wood and leaves standing around a central square, called a *batey* (BAH-teh), where public meetings or religious events took place. Inside the house, *hamaca* (AH-mah-kah), or hammocks, were hung up at night for sleeping. In the day, space was cleared for the weaving, cooking, and other work chiefly done by women.

The men made weapons, hunted, and carved small stone figures. They went about unclothed, while the women wore a cotton skirt called the *nagua* (NAH-wah).

The Taino Arawak worshiped a small pantheon of gods, with two major figures representing good and evil. Each village was dominated by a chief, or cacique. Below him was a group of nobles or privileged men who had several wives and were exempt from the more laborious tasks of village life. Further down in rank were the ordinary men, and at the lowest level of society were the workers or slaves.

The *jíbaro* remind Puerto Ricans today of an older, simpler lifestyle and of the values of honesty and independence.

EL JÍBARO

The *jíbaro* (HEE-bah-row) are traditionally farmers descended from runaway slaves or deserters from Spanish rule. The *jíbaro* lived in the mountainous interior of Puerto Rico. Their homes, called *bohío* (boh-HEE-oh), were simple palm-thatched structures. Like the Taino Arawak, they slept in hammocks hung from the ceiling that were cleared away during the day to make space for other activities.

The *jíbaro* spent most of the day working in the fields and sang old Spanish songs with their neighbors in the evening. They made a living growing subsistence crops, such as plantain, banana, yam, and *yuca* (YOO-kah), or cassava. They also kept chickens and pigs. Their religion mixed Catholicism with Taino Arawak and African beliefs.

There are few *jíbaro* still living and farming in Puerto Rico. Many of them have moved to towns, where they live in concrete houses with electricity and work in factories.

TRADITIONAL *JÍBARO* DRESS

If any style of dress reflects traditional Puerto Rican dress, it is the simple attire of the *jíbaro*, the peasant farmer.

A wide-rimmed straw hat known as a *pava* (PAH-vah) keeps the sun out of his eyes as the *jíbaro* harvests the crops. He wears a loose-fitting rough cotton shirt and trousers and usually moves around barefoot. On sugar-cane plantations, the *jíbaro* carries a machete for cutting the cane and undergrowth.

Traditional *jíbaro* dress for women has a Spanish look—a low-necked peasant blouse, a long, full cotton dirndl skirt, and a headscarf, all in bright colors, with lots of chunky jewelry and hoop earrings.

URBANIZATION

Puerto Rico is the most urbanized country in the Caribbean. Economic and social progress over the past 50 years has increased employment opportunities and standards of living, propelling a great migration in the country. Puerto Ricans have moved from the rural areas to towns in search of jobs and better lives.

About three-quarters of Puerto Ricans live in cities and urban centers today, compared to two-thirds living on farms and in the countryside 60 years ago. Although young Puerto Ricans are mostly well-educated city dwellers, many come from families who still remember living a rural peasant lifestyle.

Puerto Rico's population of nearly 4 million is very unevenly distributed. About half live on the northern coast and about one-third in San Juan and its surrounding satellite towns. The three towns of Bayamón, Guaynabo, and Carolina are within 10 miles (16 km) of San Juan, and many of their residents commute to San Juan.

Despite the rural-to-urban migration, Puerto Rico still has many tiny villages, some with fewer than 150 people, in its mountainous interior.

Skin color is often an indicator of social status in Puerto Rico. Most of the rich are light-skinned or white, and most of the poor are darker-skinned.

RACE RELATIONS

The blurring of ethnic characteristics means that there is little ethnic tension in Puerto Rico. There is no problem of racial discrimination. However, social status is linked to skin color.

In the past some families went to great lengths to preserve their racial purity, often insisting that candidates for marriage go through blood purification trials known as *limpieza de sangre* (lim-pee-EH-zah deh SAHNG-greh) to make sure they had no slave blood. However, education, health, and public places were open to anyone who could afford it.

In the late 19th century, African Puerto Ricans were leading members of society. José Celso Barbosa was a doctor who served in the cabinet as undersecretary of education in 1897. Rafael Cordero Molina, formerly a shoemaker, established a school where all poor children who came to him received a free education.

In the town of Loíza, the majority of the population are of African descent. They have not intermarried as much as in other parts of Puerto Rico, so that Loíza today is one of the purest centers of African culture on the island. On the other hand, San Juan has enclaves of exclusively white families living in wealthy areas. They are either immigrants from the United States or descendants of the Spanish colonialists.

PUERTO RICANS IN THE UNITED STATES

Several factors motivated Puerto Ricans to migrate to the United States during the 20th century. Economic depression in the 1930s fueled this migration until the mid-1960s. When the Korean War ended in 1955, a labor shortage in the United States led thousands of Puerto Ricans to look for work there, but migration slowed when job prospects were bad. During the early 1960s some Puerto Ricans returned to their homeland from the United States.

Puerto Ricans in the United States generally enjoyed a higher income and standard of living than in their homeland. How much higher, however, depended on their skin color. White-skinned Puerto Ricans tended to find jobs and good homes more easily than dark-skinned Puerto Ricans.

Most of the early migrants settled in New York City around the Brooklyn Naval Yard and Harlem. Many also settled in other parts of the city, often alongside African-Americans. They worked in the East Coast—as domestic workers and meat packers and in factories producing clothing, toys, and furniture—from January to June, then returned to Puerto Rico for the sugarcane harvest. They were poorly paid and faced extreme conditions. Some were exploited because they could not speak English.

In 2004 the United States was home to an estimated 2 million Puerto Ricans, living in New York, New Jersey, New England, Illinois, and California.

Many Puerto Ricans live in the United States. As U.S. citizens, Puerto Ricans can immigrate freely.

LIFESTYLE

THE TRADITIONAL PUERTO RICAN FAMILY is strongly religious and greatly respects social hierarchies. Puerto Rico's introduction to the 20th century was sudden. The island transformed from a poor agricultural society to a comparatively wealthy one in just 50 years, well within the memory of many of its citizens.

Puerto Rico shares certain cultural traits with other Latin American countries, particularly the concept of machismo, or a belief in male superiority. Puerto Ricans also share the Latin idea of fatalism—that life is controlled by some guiding force and misfortune is the will of God. Puerto Ricans have a strong sense of dignity and respect, and yet also a fun-loving nature. They love being in the company of other people, and being alone too much seems very odd to them.

Left: **A recreation of Taino Arawak village life.**

Opposite: **A Puerto Rican family feeds pigeons in San Juan.**

Strong family ties are typical in Puerto Rican society, especially in rural areas. Children are cherished and often spoiled by doting parents.

THE FAMILY

Of all the economic and social developments that have changed Puerto Rican society in the last 50 years, the biggest have been in the family structure. The traditional Puerto Rican family followed a strict Latin structure. The father was the undisputed head of the family and made family decisions, often without consulting his wife or children. The wife was a silent partner in the marriage but was respected by her children and honored by her husband.

Boys were traditionally preferred to girls. A husband who was unable to produce a male heir would be called a *chancletero* (shahn-cleh-TEH-roh), an expression meaning a maker of useless things. Boys were taught to uphold the concept of machismo, while girls were protected from outside influences for the honor of the family. A girl's virginity was very important to family honor, to be protected at all costs. A young woman might meet her boyfriend in chaperoned outings but never alone. Even wives would not go out alone.

At the opposite extreme are Puerto Rican families in New York City, almost half of which are headed by single women, the others being

PUERTO RICAN NAMES

Like some North Americans, Puerto Ricans have three names, but two are surnames. The first name is their given or Christian name, the second their father's surname, and the third their mother's maiden name. Confusion often arises when Puerto Ricans and North Americans meet, because North Americans may assume that the last name is the surname. They might say "Hello Senor Acosta" to a man whose name is José López Acosta, when his surname is López, his father's surname. Puerto Ricans who are not used to such mistakes are sometimes upset at being called by their mother's surname.

When women marry, they may choose to drop their mother's surname before taking their husband's surname. If Margot Ruiz Marchessi marries a man whose surname is Betances, her full name may be either Margot Ruiz Betances or Margot Ruiz Marchessi de Betances. To avoid confusion, many Puerto Ricans in the United States have stopped using their mother's surname.

combinations of members from previous marriages, that is, half-brothers and half-sisters living with divorced and remarried parents.

The typical modern Puerto Rican family lies somewhere in between these two extremes. Family roles and responsibilities are less rigid and more shared. Women have equal opportunities in education and more freedom of movement. They earn half the family income, take part in family decision making, plan their family size, and have the right to divorce if they decide their marriage is not successful.

Exposure to North American culture has significantly changed the perspective and lifestyle of modern Puerto Rican women living in the cities. They have their own career and aspirations—material comfort, mobility, and the best for their children. However, Puerto Rican girls still face many social restrictions. For example, although dating is no longer chaperoned, they are expected to moderate their behavior in public.

Social welfare benefits encourage Puerto Ricans to marry and start families. The lower classes, with rising economic expectations, want more middle-class lifestyles. Family remains very important to Puerto Ricans. Family members tend to do things together, and any occasion can be an excuse for the family to get together. Departures and arrivals at the airport are often attended by family members saying goodbye to the traveler or welcoming them home.

The barrio once provided an important social support system for the family and community.

THE EXTENDED FAMILY

The support of extended families has always been important to Latin Americans. It was customary for several generations to live together to survive the hardships of war or natural disaster. Often, four generations in a family all lived under the same roof.

Although it was once an accepted part of life in Puerto Rican society that the extended family lived close by, this is becoming less common. Most people no longer live in the barrio, or neighborhood where they grew up. Instead, they live in areas close to their workplace. As a result, family members can no longer call on one another for help as easily as they did before.

Neighbors in the barrio were also traditionally an important part of society. Since different families may have lived side by side for many generations, they would also have considered themselves part of an extended family.

In an extended-family system, orphaned children would have had their relatives to turn to, or an uncle out of work would have had nieces and nephews to give him food and shelter. The elderly would have ended their days with children and grandchildren around them. Today, dependence on the extended family is less prevalent, and the nuclear family of a father, mother, and two or more children is more common. The old role of the extended family has been taken over by the state, as it has in most other Western countries.

COMPADRAZGO

Although the most important relationships were always within the extended family, an exception to the rule was, and still is, the idea of *compadrazgo* (cohm-pahd-RAZ-goh), which means coparenting.

This is similar to the concept of godparenting, where close friends or relatives stand at the parents' side at the child's baptism. In Puerto Rico, the *compadre* (cohm-PAH-dreh), or godfather, and the *comadre* (coh-MAH-dreh), or godmother, are usually family friends.

Compadrazgo relationships go beyond occasional birthday presents for the child. They are almost spiritual relationships between the parents and coparents, and are close to the Native American idea of blood brotherhood or blood sisterhood. If necessary, a *compadre* may take over the role of the father and bring up the child.

Parents and godparents will not become rivals, as their relationship implies deep respect. In the past, a poor family might ask their *patrón* (pah-TRON), or local landowner, to be the child's godparent, and the bond between them might be work on the farm in exchange for support and help in hard times.

Organizations aimed at helping new Puerto Rican families in the United States have found the idea of *compadrazgo* useful in helping immigrants settle into North American society. An already settled family is encouraged to form a *compadrazgo* relationship with a new immigrant family, and help them adjust to life in the United States.

Compadrazgo relationships bond the parents, their child, and the godparent. The godparent plays an active role in bringing up the child and attends important family gatherings.

Puerto Rico is a male-dominated society.

MACHISMO

Machismo, the belief that men are superior to women, is an integral concept in Puerto Rican society. A man is expected to display physical strength, bravery, and dominance over his wife and children. He must maintain the respect and dignity he deserves—respect and dignity that he can lose if his children are disobedient or his wife defiant or, worse, unfaithful.

Ironically, machismo can be enhanced by having extramarital affairs, although these are publicly disapproved. Girls, on the other hand, are expected to show proper behavior, seeking parental approval of one or two boyfriends, and quickly formalizing courtship to avoid a reputation for loose living.

An important part of machismo is mutual respect. This is seen in the formal language and behavior of two men in conversation. This respect has nothing to do with a man's wealth, since a poor man can expect much respect from wealthier neighbors as long as he demonstrates his dignity and pride. A man who spends his time complaining about his problems loses dignity.

Puerto Rican men may be insulted by the terms *nangotado* (nahng-goh-TAH-doh), meaning stooped, and *aplatado* (ahp-laht-AH-doh), meaning flattened out. Because of the threat to another man's dignity, or machismo, Puerto Rican men are careful to avoid open hostility or direct refusal.

POPULATION AND BIRTH CONTROL

In 1898, when Puerto Rico became a U.S. protectorate, its population stood at barely a million people. But within 40 years the population had doubled. Family size was very large, especially in rural areas—a rural family might have 10 children or more. This fast population growth worried the administration.

Until 1939 it was a felony to even offer advice on contraception in Puerto Rico. Until the 1960s it was considered a sin to do so in this Roman Catholic country. However, the Family Planning Association was set up in 1948, and by the late 1960s it had 60 centers all over the island providing free family-planning advice and contraceptives to more than 30,000 women.

The big breakthrough in attempts to control the population came in 1968 after the election of Governor Luis A. Ferré. Birth control information and subsidized contraceptives were made available in government health centers. Today, family size is related to education and income level. Middle-class families have two or three children, while lower-class families may have six children.

Different standards of behavior apply to relationships between men and women. While machismo leads to greater tolerance for promiscuity in men, women are expected to be virtuous and seek serious marriage partners. Protective fathers with machismo values may not allow daughters to date for too long before settling down.

An increase in the number of women working has altered the traditional structure of Puerto Rico's society and way of life, especially in the cities.

OTHER VALUES

Fatalism has a big influence in traditional Puerto Rican culture. Fatalism is the belief that life is controlled by supernatural forces and that people should accept their fate. Good fortune should be accepted gladly, but if misfortune occurs that too should be accepted without complaint.

For the rich in Puerto Rican society, this can justify wealth, while the poor comfort themselves by saying that misfortune is the will of God. But like other Latin values, this is being eroded by modern institutions, such as trade unions, and by the breakup of the old landowner-worker relationship.

Another strong belief among Latin men is *personalismo* (per-son-ahl-IZ-moh)—the individual worth of each man. This idea works against group activities, such as trade unionism. Individuals will often put their trust in one powerful man rather than in a group of peers. People in Puerto Rico tend to support and vote for individuals rather than sets of ideas belonging to one political party or another. This characteristic also leads to a strong preference for personal contact, especially in business.

Puerto Ricans believe in bending rules to suit the circumstances. A common expression, *ay bendito* (aye ben-DEE-toh), which literally means blessed be the Lord, is also used to mean something like "have a heart." It is often used with traffic policemen by people caught speeding who want to avoid being fined.

These Puerto Rican values and characteristics are often quite difficult for North Americans to appreciate. The concept of *personalismo* and a belief in bending rules make many Western business practices, with their rules and regulations, quite foreign to Puerto Ricans.

LIFE IN THE COUNTRYSIDE

About two generations ago, two-thirds of Puerto Ricans lived in the countryside, visiting the nearest pueblo, or small town, for shopping. The traditional rural inhabitant was the *jíbaro*. Today, less than one-third of Puerto Ricans live in rural areas, though in the island's interior there are still many small farming villages and communities that are far removed from city life.

Life in the countryside is slow, with the traditional protective attitudes to women and girls. The work is physically hard, and as agricultural work is poorly paid there is no middle class.

Traditionally, the Puerto Rican rural community existed on subsistence crops, supplemented by work on the local landowners' fields. After 1898, when U.S. corporations bought up the sugar plantations and turned them into large-scale businesses, the structure of rural life changed. The independent *jíbaro* could no longer negotiate with his *patrón*, since the new landowners were corporations in the United States.

Rural society changed quickly into large groups of laborers who negotiated collectively with foremen, especially in the coastal plains that were more profitable to farm. But in the mountainous areas where coffee plantations are cultivated, the traditional lifestyle remains.

Puerto Ricans have one of the highest ratios of cars to adults in the world, which makes driving in the city hazardous. There are many public buses and a system of nontraditional transportation, in which fares can be negotiated.

An exclusive residential neighborhood in San Juan.

CITY LIFE

A large middle class can be found in cities and towns, living comfortable lives with good employment prospects. The capital is surrounded by a number of satellite towns from which residents can easily commute to work. Like North American cities, San Juan has shopping malls, convenience stores, leisure centers, parks, and other amenities. Houses in San Juan are designed for nuclear families, with carports and yards. Land has become the largest factor in the cost of a home, and housing developments now include many apartment complexes and low-cost housing projects designed to house the poor. There are also exclusive and expensive complexes with carefully protected doors and windows.

Many Puerto Ricans who live in cities have kept up their ties to their rural roots, and a regular weekend or vacation activity is to travel into the countryside to visit relatives. Most families own a car, and there is an efficient public transportation system that travels across the mountains and into the small villages.

SHANTYTOWNS

In the past 40 years, the massive internal migration of Puerto Ricans to cities and towns has resulted in the development of *arrabales* (ah-rah-BAH-yes), meaning slums or shantytowns.

One shantytown in San Juan is La Perla, built on a public beach and separated from the city by the old city walls. This brightly colored settlement is a tourist attraction in the capital. With housing shortages and high costs in the city, there is little point in evicting the squatters of La Perla, since they at least have a community to live in there. They are mostly unemployed and living on welfare payments, but many have refrigerators, television sets, and cars. The government provides La Perla with water and electricity, building materials, and garbage collection services.

HEALTH CARE

When the first Puerto Rican men were called up to serve in the U.S. Army in World War II, more than 78 percent of them failed the medical test. At that time, the general health of Puerto Ricans was poor, as most of them could not afford health care. In 1940 there was only one doctor for every 4,000 citizens.

Since then, great improvements in health care have been made. The number of doctors has increased, and hospitals and clinics have been set up in towns and rural areas. Much of Puerto Rico's health care is covered by medical insurance, while Medicaid helps the needy pay their medical bills. Another reason for the better health record is that diet has also improved enormously.

Improved health care has increased Puerto Rican life expectancy from 47 years in 1940 to 77.5 years in 2004.

A shanty house on Guajataca Beach. Shanties are built from corrugated iron and wood, often with no sanitation. Unfortunately, some of these slums have also become centers of drugs and crime.

73

EDUCATION

During the early years of U.S. rule, the American governors of Puerto Rico believed that the English language and U.S. culture were the keys to the island's future. English was made the language of instruction in schools, despite the fact that neither the teachers nor the pupils could understand or speak it. In 1948 the United States handed over the administration of the island's education system to a locally appointed commissioner of education. Spanish was then officially restored as the language of instruction, and English became compulsory as a second language. Today the ability to speak English is essential in most jobs in Puerto Rico, and most people in the cities and towns are bilingual.

The Puerto Rican government has invested heavily in raising educational levels in Puerto Rico. As a result, Puerto Ricans are among the most educated people in the Caribbean. The island's literacy rate has risen above 90 percent, compared to 69 percent in 1940.

THE YOUNG LORDS

In the mid-1960s, when students virtually all over the world discovered the effectiveness of student protest, Puerto Rican students in Puerto Rico and in major cities in the United States discovered that they could make a point by demonstrating.

One such group active in New York City were the Young Lords, who became concerned with the lack of educational opportunities for young Puerto Ricans. On one occasion they occupied a New York City church and used it to set up an early morning educational program for children. For a while, another group of Young Lords caused the City University of New York to close for a period in 1969.

Their efforts brought the plight of Puerto Rican students to the public's attention, made Puerto Rican voters aware that they could influence the educational system, and helped bring about bilingual programs in the city. They were also responsible for the establishment of several Puerto Rican study programs in the universities around New York City.

Puerto Rico's education system has undergone enormous change, from education for the privileged few to almost universal primary education. A large proportion of the population graduates from high school. Changing educational standards have resulted in an increasing number of college graduates in Puerto Rico. The island has more than 50 institutions of higher learning and one of the highest college attendance rates—more than 50 percent—in the world.

There are many flourishing private schools on the island that have a high success rate in getting students into the government-run university. Ironically, poorer students who are educated in the public school system get poorer grades and lose out on acceptance in the University of Puerto Rico. They then must seek places at the less prestigious but more expensive private colleges.

A new problem in the Puerto Rican education system is teaching Spanish to the children of returned emigrants.

Education is the key to a better life in Puerto Rico. About 80 percent of working Puerto Ricans have more than 13 years of education, while 70 percent of the unemployed have less than 12 years of education.

LIFE IN THE UNITED STATES

Almost 40 percent of all people of Puerto Rican descent live in the United States. For some Puerto Ricans, life in the United States is just a temporary measure to make enough money or provide their children with a good education. When these are satisfied, they return to Puerto Rico to live. Second-generation Puerto Ricans who were born in New York City but have returned to the island are called Nuyoricans.

Many Puerto Ricans who have become disillusioned with life in the United States have returned only to find that their children feel homesick for the American lifestyle. Many of these have problems adapting to the language and culture of their ancestry. Puerto Ricans who have settled permanently in the United States find that the second generation has to adjust between North American culture at school and the culture of their parents at home.

Puerto Rican women who are housewives in the United States may face the most difficulties in adjusting to the new culture. While their husbands and children adapt through the workplace or through school, housewives often remain in a largely Spanish-speaking neighborhood.

Many schools in New York City have introduced bilingual teaching programs to make sure that Puerto Rican students are not disadvantaged. Although many students

Puerto Ricans make up one-fourth of all students in New York City's public schools. New York City has the greatest concentration of Puerto Ricans in the United States.

are now third-generation New Yorkers, the percentage of Puerto Ricans who graduate is still below the national average. California has the highest level of Puerto Ricans in professional and managerial positions, and the highest incomes among Puerto Ricans in the United States.

UNEMPLOYMENT

With around 12 percent of Puerto Rico's population unemployed, welfare payments have long been a large public-expenditure item in Puerto Rico. The U.S. government contributes to welfare payments in Puerto Rico, though this support is less than that received by states such as Mississippi. U.S. food stamps and Medicaid are supplemented by the Puerto Rican government. Puerto Rico's welfare payments would be brought up to U.S. standards if Puerto Rico joined the union. Unemployed Puerto Ricans would then receive bigger welfare checks.

In rural areas, many people prefer welfare to low-paid work.

Though welfare payments to unemployed Puerto Ricans are low by U.S. standards, they keep the island's unemployment rate high. There is little incentive to find work, since people lose their welfare rights as soon as they get a job, even a low-paying one.

Another aspect of Puerto Rico's unemployment problem is the creation of new manufacturing jobs. With the removal of Section 936, the loss of jobs put the burden of maintaining the economy on other industries, such as tourism, making their development very important to controlling unemployment and the number of welfare dependents.

RELIGION

ALTHOUGH PUERTO RICO is mainly a Roman Catholic country, its religious beliefs have been influenced by those of the Taino Arawak and by the spiritualism that the African slaves practiced. These influences make Puerto Rican Catholicism different from Catholicism elsewhere. Worship of individual saints is also much stronger and more common in Puerto Rico than in other Catholic countries.

The Catholic faith first came to Puerto Rico with Spanish settlers. Spanish priests later spread the faith to the indigenous people and converted them. Catholicism spread quickly throughout the island in the 17th century. Thatched-roof churches were built in every settlement, and the church became as prominent a building in the town square as the municipal hall.

Above: **Four centuries of Spanish rule have led to a predominantly Roman Catholic population in Puerto Rico.**

Opposite: **The Cathedral of Our Lady of Guadalupe in Ponce, Puerto Rico's second largest city.**

INDIGENOUS BELIEFS

The Taino Arawak believed in a supreme creator, Yocahu, who lived high in the central range on the mountain now called El Yunque. They believed in a spirit world in which all living things had souls, and rivers, trees, and stones had spirits living in them.

The equivalent of the devil in the religion of the Taino Arawak was called *jurakan* (hoo-rah-KAHN). He could call forth terrible powers of nature to harm the people. It is from the word *jurakan* that the English word hurricane is derived.

AFRICAN INFLUENCE

When slaves were brought to the island of Puerto Rico from Africa, they took with them some elements of their religion, including a kind of animism. Vestiges of their spirituality are still present in the religious festivals of the Puerto Rican town of Loíza, where masqueraders wear masks and costumes similar to those worn by the Yoruba people of Nigeria.

Puerto Rico's indigenous people also worshiped lesser gods called *cemi* (SAY-mee). Each family or village had a carved wooden or stone image of their own *cemi*. The Taino Arawak believed in the afterlife and buried their dead carefully, equipping their graves with food, water, weapons, and jewelry. Some of their spiritual beliefs are still seen in the practices of the *jíbaro*.

THE CHURCH AND LIFE'S BIG EVENTS

In 2004, 85 percent of the Puerto Rican population was Roman Catholic. Most practice a very personal form of the faith. Unlike in other Catholic countries of Latin America, Mass and confession are not a big part of the faith in Puerto Rico. Instead most homes have pictures or statues of particular saints whom the family call on when they need help and protection. A person may turn to the Virgin Mary for comfort in times of trouble and keep a statue for protection.

In daily life, Puerto Ricans use religious expressions very often, such as *Si Dios quiere* (see dee-OH kee-AIR-eh), meaning God willing, or *ay bendito* (aye ben-DEE-toh), meaning blessed be the Lord.

Most Puerto Rican children are baptized in church by a priest, and parents will often look for someone to form a *compadrazgo* relationship with their child. Growing up, Puerto Rican children are surrounded by statues representing the holy family and the saints, and are taught

to beware *el diablo* (el dee-AH-bloh), the devil. At age 7, children make their first Holy Communion. At puberty, they are confirmed in the Church with an additional name, usually that of a saint for whom they have developed a special reverence.

Church weddings are common among wealthier families in Puerto Rico. Among the poor, common-law marriages not formalized by the church also take place. Children born within common-law marriages can still be baptized in a church.

Puerto Ricans also seek blessings when they start a new business. Whenever a new shop or office opens, priests are called upon to perform a blessing at the opening ceremony.

Among the other religions in Puerto Rico is Judaism. San Juan has a small Jewish community of a few hundred families.

OTHER FORMS OF CHRISTIANITY

The Roman Catholic Church's emphasis on suffering life's adversities and being rewarded for goodness in heaven rather than on earth explains why people in Latin American countries have suffered poverty without much complaint. Protestant values, on the other hand, indicate that reward can come while still on earth, and that hard work should be followed by material happiness.

Considered heretical by the Catholic Church, Protestantism was not allowed in any of the Catholic colonies until the 19th century. The first Protestant churches were established in Ponce and on Vieques, after Queen Victoria of Britain asked for special dispensation for English families who had settled there. Later, an Episcopalian church was set up by North Americans settling in Puerto Rico.

DEATH CUSTOMS

Death is marked both by a religious service and by personal customs. In rural areas, dying people receive the church's last rites and are also visited by their friends and neighbors, who keep a night-long *velada* (veh-LAH-dah), or vigil, during the person's final hours. The *velada* is held in the home of the dying person, with the women inside the house and the men outside. After a death, another night-long *velada* is held, also with the men outside and the women inside. Food and cane rum might be served, but the event never becomes loud. In some regions, the rosary is said for nine nights following the funeral service, which is conducted by a priest.

In the cities, as with other events, the observance of a death is more like a funeral in North America. A religious service is followed by a brief family gathering at the home of the deceased.

After the U.S. takeover in 1898, Protestant communities in the United States saw Puerto Rico as a field for conversions. Today, Puerto Rico has about half a million Protestants, most belonging to one of the revivalist movements. Among the churches represented in Puerto Rico are the Methodists, Baptists, Episcopalians, Jehovah's Witnesses, and Mormons.

The Pentecostal church has also found support in Puerto Rico. This church practices faith healing, and members seek to become one with the Holy Spirit. Meetings are small, often held in homes or local stores. There is lively singing, and members are encouraged to share their faith. Some may feel they have been taken over by the Holy Spirit and may manifest certain signs of the experience, such as speaking in tongues, which is usually unintelligible to the hearer and sounds like ecstatic speech. Members of the Pentecostal church are encouraged to abstain from drinking and smoking and to obey certain dress codes. The pastors of Puerto Rico's Pentecostal churches often come from the local population rather than from the United States.

The Roman Catholic San Juan Church.

Puerto Rico also has a homegrown form of evangelism, which developed in the 1940s around a woman named Mita. Mita saw the improvement of conditions for her congregation as part of her mission on earth. She died in 1970, but her sect lives on. It has opened churches in New York City and Chicago, and runs businesses and provides work opportunities for its members.

SPIRITUALISM

Spiritualism exists in Puerto Rico along with the more established religions. Puerto Rico's Christians combine their spiritualist tradition with their Christian practices.

Every town or city in Puerto Rico has at least one spirit medium who may be a housewife, a truck driver, or a member of a profession, and who is believed to have special powers to contact the spirits of the dead to ask for protection and guidance, and to predict the future. Spiritualists even call on the pillars of the Catholic Church, such as the saints, for guidance. Their homes are often filled with pictures and statues of saints and other religious figures. Seekers of spiritualists come from all levels of society, from rich to poor.

Other spiritualists use natural medicine to help the sick. In every town, shops called *botánica* (boh-TAHN-ih-kah) sell herbal medicines used by spiritualists. Some of the herbs are harmless, others can be dangerous. Several have been studied by modern medicine and found to be cures for the ailments for which the spiritualists prescribe them. Medicines can be made into herbal teas called *tisanas* (tih-SAHN-ahs) or mixed with alcohol as a rub.

These shops also sell candles, incense, and other things associated with the Catholic Church, as well as charms, amulets, magic powders, and other things not associated with the Catholic Church. They are equally popular in New York and other U.S. cities with Puerto Rican neighborhoods, where they attract a wide variety of people from all classes of life, including born-and-bred New Yorkers.

Some old spiritual beliefs and ceremonies include the *rosario* (roh-ZAHR-ee-oh), where a shrine is set up for a sick person and the family and neighbors pray to the saints to help the person recover. Another

Among simpler people on the island, a belief in the evil eye still exists. Babies wear an amulet of black beads to protect them from harm.

traditional spiritualist ceremony is the *rogativa* (roh-gah-TEE-vah), where a whole neighborhood turns out in the street to pray for a need. If there is a drought, for example, everyone joins together to pray for rain.

In remote areas of the island, particularly around Loíza, there are more obvious signs of the religions of the African ancestors. People carry with them a *resurgado* (reh-zer-GAHR-doh), or talisman, that keeps the evil eye or witchcraft away. In the old days, simple people believed in love potions or spells, but the influence of modern medicines and satellite television has caused the disappearance of many of those old beliefs.

A wall mural shows a masked figure from African tradition in a Christian ceremony.

¡ Lo Mejor De San Juan !

Galería Café

SOPAS Y ENSALADA

DESAYUNOS

SANDWICHES Y HAMBURGERS

REFRESCOS

JUGOS Y BATIDAS DE FRUTAS NATURALES

VINOS   JAMONES

QUESOS

BANDEJAS DE ENTREMESES

Y MUCHO MAS...

LANGUAGE

UNTIL U.S. RULE, language was a simple affair in Puerto Rico. No one spoke English. Everyone spoke a form of Spanish that had certain differences from the Spanish that was spoken in Spain but that could be understood. When the first U.S. soldiers tried to communicate with Puerto Ricans, they used mainly nods, smiles, and basic sign language.

Today English has become the passport to job success in Puerto Rico. It is learned in school, from television, and on the streets. An interesting product of mixing Spanish and English is Spanglish, a lively dialect formulated on the streets of New York City and introduced by returning Puerto Ricans. It is a mixture of Spanish grammar, English vocabulary, and some New York City street talk.

SPANGLISH

Spanglish is an odd mixture of English and Spanish that evolved among Latin American communities in the United States. It is made up of words borrowed from English, mostly either slang words or technical words describing some new idea or object.

Some words borrowed from English date back from before 1898, such as *ron* (rohn), the Spanish word for rum that came from the British Antilles in the 1870s. Another English word, foxtrot, the name of a dance that was popular in the 1920s, has entered Puerto Rican Spanish and now means fight.

Then there are other English words, such as bar, record, ticket, and standard, that have moved whole into Spanglish. An even more interesting effect of bilingualism and Spanglish is the way Puerto Ricans use two languages in one sentence, such as "*se está* brushing his teeth" ("he is brushing his teeth") or "*tu miras* funny" ("you look funny").

Te invita a presenciar los VIII Juegos Panamericanos de Silla de Ruedas

...gilla • Mayagüez,
...uerto Rico
...de noviembre de

NORBERTO VELAZQUEZ
Atleta Símbolo

de los VIII Juegos Panam...

El Ana...

A poster advertising the Invalid Games for Puerto Ricans uses Spanish, the official language.

SPANISH

The wave of Spanish colonization in the Caribbean and South America in the 16th century meant that Spanish was the dominant language of the region. Even today, people in Central America, some West Indian islands, and the Caribbean coast of South America still speak a form of Spanish. The accent and pronunciation in these former Spanish colonies differ from those in Spain, but the language is still recognizable as Spanish.

Puerto Rican Spanish has its own unique characteristics. One of its features is that many consonants that should be pronounced in Spanish by using the front of the mouth, are softened and pronounced in the back of the mouth. For example, the rolled *r* formed in Spanish by flicking the tongue against the back of the teeth, has become softer sounding, like in French. Another example is that the letter *s* is not pronounced, which makes it difficult for a foreigner to tell if the person is speaking in the singular or plural. In Puerto Rico, the word *gracias* sounds like *grahiah* (GRAH-hee-ah), and *las madres*, meaning the mothers, sounds like *la madre* (lah MAH-dreh), meaning the mother. Similarly, the double *l* in some Spanish words is pronounced like an English-sounding *y*. For example, *tortilla* sounds like tor-TEE-yah.

Another interesting feature of Puerto Rican Spanish is that words ending in *-ado* are sometimes pronounced without the *d* sound. It is a question of class, the dropped *d* being the common pronunciation and the inserted *d* being the formal pronunciation.

Some words whose origin is uniquely Puerto Rican are *pon* (pohn), meaning hitchhike, *chevere* (shey-VAIR-eh), meaning well done, and *agallarse* (ahg-ahl-YAR-seh), meaning to become angry.

Unlike other Caribbean countries, such as Jamaica, where pidgin dialects have emerged, Puerto Rican Spanish is still very much like Spanish spoken elsewhere in the world. It can still be understood by a Spanish speaker from outside the country.

USTED AND TU

Different languages have different ways of expressing politeness and respect. In many languages, the speaker shows respect for someone by using appropriate titles to address the person, such as "sir" or "ma'am," or polite request words such as "please."

One way of expressing politeness and respect that does not exist in English but is very important in Spanish is in the variations of the word you. In Spanish, *usted* (oo-STEH) is used in the plural and *tu* (too) in the singular. But *usted* is also used to show respect. For example, in a *compadrazgo* relationship, which is formal in nature, both parties show each other respect by using the word *usted*. However, when close friends speak informally, they can use *tu*.

TAINO ARAWAK INFLUENCES

Before the language of the Taino Arawak influenced that of the Spanish settlers, it had infiltrated the language of their Carib attackers. Legend has it that the Carib captured Taino Arawak women during their attacks on the Taino Arawak. These women, although living with the Carib, still spoke their own language and taught it to their daughters, who stayed at home with them. Their sons, who went out to work with their Carib fathers, learned the language of the Carib. As a result, the Carib had two languages—one spoken by the women and another by the men.

A bus stop street sign in San Juan.

The names of many Puerto Rican towns, such as Mayagüez, Manatí, and Arecibo, are of Taino Arawak origin, and the town of Caguas is named after a Taino Arawak chief, Caguax, who once ruled over the valley where the town is now located.

Some words have come from the Taino Arawak language, been absorbed into Spanish, and subsequently entered the English language. The English word hurricane comes from the Taino Arawak word *jurakan*, and the word hammock comes from the Taino Arawak word *hamaca*. Other words of Taino Arawak origin include tobacco, canoe, maracas, savannah, and key, meaning small island, as in Florida Keys.

It is believed that about 500 words, many to do with plants and animals, in Puerto Rican Spanish are of Taino Arawak origin. The word *guajana* (goo-ah-CHAR-nah) describes the tips of the sugarcane stalk and is a word found only in Puerto Rico, unlike many other Taino Arawak words found in the Dominican Republic, Cuba, and other former Spanish colonies in the Caribbean that once had Taino Arawak populations.

A roadside snack bar advertises its wares.

AFRICAN WORDS

The language of the West African slaves whom the Spanish brought to Puerto Rico has also had a lasting effect on the island's dialect.

Although the African slaves survived much longer under Spanish rule than did the Taino Arawak, the African influence on the Spanish language was minimal. One theory to explain this is that the Spanish took slaves from different tribes in various areas of Africa. These groups might not have spoken the same language, and the only language they had in common was probably the Spanish they learned from their masters.

Some African words that survive in the language of Puerto Ricans today are *bemebe* (bay-MEH-bay), which means big lip, *quimbombo* (keem-BOM-boh), which means okra, and *guneo* (goo-NEY-oh), which means banana. The name of a ceremony that takes place after the death of an infant, *baquine* (bah-KEEN-eh), is also of African origin, as is the ceremony itself.

Above: **Road signs in English and Spanish cater to a bilingual population.**

Opposite: **A young boy delivers newspapers.**

THE ADVENT OF ENGLISH

In 1898 virtually no one in Puerto Rico spoke English. The U.S. administration in Puerto Rico set about changing this by introducing English in schools.

Under the Clark Policy (named after the first education commissioner, Victor Clark), English was made the language of instruction in schools, even though the teachers and pupils spoke no English and had no English textbooks.

Since then various methods have introduced bilingualism to the country. For a time Spanish was the language of instruction in the lower grades in school, with both languages being used in the middle grades, and English in the higher grades. Today Spanish is the language of instruction in schools, and English is taught as a foreign language in daily lessons.

More and more Puerto Ricans are bilingual in English and Spanish. English proficiency enables them to further their education or succeed in business. Private schools promote their English-language courses by pointing out the economic advantage of speaking English. In 1997 the government introduced a plan to emphasize the teaching of English in schools. However, language policy is a sensitive issue in a nation that seeks to balance its need to compete in the English-speaking world of business, with its need to preserve the language of its culture.

A newer language problem has surfaced as Puerto Rican families return from the United States. Their children are often more proficient in English than Spanish, and this has stimulated the provision of extra classes in Spanish.

THE PRESS

Several newspapers are published in English or Spanish in Puerto Rico. The most radical newspaper is *Claridad*, which began as the mouthpiece of the pro-independence movement. Its readership has grown over the years with several important stories on scandals in the government and the private sector. *Claridad* is read largely by younger Puerto Ricans and by supporters of Communism.

El Nuevo Día is a conservative and pro-statehood Spanish-language tabloid that covers lots of gossip and book excerpts. The English-language *San Juan Star*, read mainly by the English-speaking and expatriate community, is mildly pro-statehood, and much of its coverage is North American.

Several newspapers from the United States are also available in Puerto Rico, including *The Washington Post*, *The New York Times*, and *El Diario*.

ARTS

PUERTO RICO'S STRONG artistic tradition has been shaped by its Taino Arawak, Spanish, and African heritage. Cultural traditions are preserved in its daily life, the media, museums, and the lively contributions of writers and musicians. The arts of Puerto Rico have also influenced the arts in the United States through the island's emigrants and its close economic and political association with the United States.

FOLK ART

Traditional Puerto Rican handicrafts include hammocks, festival masks, carvings of saints, and tatted cloth.

Vejigante (veh-GAHN-teh) masks are made from coconuts or wood for the season of Lent. They were originally made to scare people into repentance. The Puerto Ricans later adapted them as symbols of anti-colonialism. *Vejigante* masks combine Puerto Rico's Spanish, African, and indigenous traditions, and make attractive souvenirs for tourists.

Another Puerto Rican folk handicraft is tatting, a technique similar to macramé. Threads of twine are drawn into patterns and knotted together to produce a lacy effect. The traditional hammock of the Taino Arawak has been given this treatment. Shops in San Juan display beautifully patterned hammocks detailed with tatted borders of delicate lacework. The tatted borders are called *mundillos* (moon-DEE-johs). Tatting is common around Aguadilla on the northwestern coast.

Above: **Carved *vejigante* masks.**

Opposite: **Woven baskets and dyed pampas grasses are displayed at a handicraft store in San Juan.**

The art of leatherworking came from the Spaniards. Cattle rearing was once a major industry in Puerto Rico, and leather items are still made by local craftsmen, mainly for the tourist industry. Craft shops in San Juan sell locally made leather products along with imported ones.

Musical instruments are a flourishing craft in Puerto Rico. Besides the *tres* (trehs), *cuatro* (coo-AH-troh), or *seis* (sehs), which are guitars with three, four, or six strings, local craftsmen make the traditional percussion instruments of the Taino Arawak, such as the *quiros* (KEE-rohs), *güiro* (GWEE-roh), and *claves* (CLAH-vehz).

The Taino Arawak also carved wooden boxes and bowls, and wooden thrones called *dubos* (doo-hohs) for their chiefs. They invented the hammock, using woven and dyed cloth. Taino Arawak art has been found in stone carvings dating back more than 500 years.

Puerto Rican families keep a number of *santos* (SAHN-tohs), or wooden carvings of saints, often handed down from generation to generation. Just about every saint in Christianity is represented somewhere on the island.

Some of the best *santos* in Puerto Rico are found at the Capilla del Cristo in Old San Juan. Older *santos* exhibit a delicate Spanish style, while newer ones show more of the indigenous folk style. These are often decorated with small silver medallions in the shape of parts of the body. The medallions have been put on the *santos* by people who attribute their recovery from certain illnesses to the healing powers of particular saints.

Above: **Few young people are learning the dying art of carving saint figures.**

Opposite: **A modern painting reproduces Taino Arawak art.**

Above: **A dance troupe wearing Taino Arawak ceremonial dress.**

Opposite: ***Bomba*** **dancers dance to African-influenced music and rhythm.**

MUSIC AND DANCE

Puerto Rican music evolved from Spanish dances and songs and was influenced by the rhythm of African music brought by slaves. Much of the essential sound of Puerto Rican music has Taino Arawak and African roots.

The Taino Arawak made rhythmic music using percussion instruments. They beat hollowed-out tree trunks with sticks and shook gourds filled with beans or pebbles, which they called maracas. The distinctive sound of maracas can still be heard in modern Puerto Rican music. Another Taino Arawak instrument, the *güiro*, is a carved and notched gourd played by drawing a stick across it.

The Spaniards danced to songs in the *danza* (DAHN-zah) style, similar to ballroom dancing. This was most popular in the 19th century and was performed by an orchestra with string and wind instruments. Puerto Rico's national anthem, *La Borinqueña*, is a *danza* that has been adapted to solemn music. The peasant version of this Spanish-style music, called the *danzón* (dahn-ZON), is more uptempo. This music evolved in the early 20th century, under the influence of other Latin American countries, into dance tunes such as the mazurka, merengue, and mambo.

In modern times Puerto Rico's major musical contribution has been in salsa. The person who probably did most to create this sound was Tito Puente (1923–2000). He was born in Spanish Harlem in New York City to Puerto Rican parents. Characteristic of his work, and of all salsa music, is the use of the *timbales* (tim-BAH-les), or open-ended drums played with untapered sticks. Salsa is typically full of African rhythm. Puente recorded many albums and became a legend throughout the United States and the Caribbean.

Younger salsa musicians include Willie Colón, Hector Lavoe, Willie Rosarion, and the Fania All Stars. A pop version of salsa was performed by Menudo, a teenage boy band that was successful in the 1980s in the United States and Central and South America.

In classical music, Puerto Rico's Pablo Casals was a world-famous cellist. He was born in Spain to a Puerto Rican mother and settled in Puerto Rico in 1957 at the age of 81. He instituted a world music festival in Puerto Rico that continued after his death in 1973. He also founded a music conservatory and a symphony orchestra that are among the best in the Caribbean.

Justino Díaz is one of the leading bass singers in the New York Metropolitan Opera. He is Puerto Rico's finest male vocalist and has sung all over the world.

There are several types of traditional music that are played at certain events in Puerto Rico. *Bomba* (bom-bah) and *plena* (PLAY-nyah) originated in Africa and were brought into the mainstream in Puerto Rico by Rafael Cortijo (1928–82). With his band, he experimented with these rhythmic African musical forms using modern instruments such as trumpets.

Décima (DEH-see-mah), a form of improvised poetic verse with Spanish origins, can be accompanied by three-, four-, or six-stringed guitars. It follows a structure of 10 rhyming verses, each consisting of eight syllables.

Although much of Puerto Rico's fine art is best appreciated in San Juan, the rural community is not neglected. Under a government project called Operación Serenidad, a traveling library and a mobile museum go from town to town, and a theater on wheels brings drama to remote villages. The Institute of Puerto Rican Culture also sponsors concerts, lectures, ballets, art exhibitions, plays, and films all over the island.

FINE ARTS

The first Puerto Rican painter to gain international recognition was José Campeche (1751–1809). He lived in the tiny fortress town of San Juan, painting religious paintings and commissions from local dignitaries. He created thousands of oil paintings, but few have survived. Two of his religious paintings are in the museum at Ponce, while his portrait of Governor Ustariz hangs in the Institute of Puerto Rican Culture in San Juan. The Museum of the University of Puerto Rico in Río Piedras exhibits the best of Puerto Rican art. Due to space constraints, its galleries can showcase only a fifth of its vast collection at any one time. However, the displays, ranging from pre-Columbian to contemporary, are always splendid.

Francisco Oller y Cestero (1833–1917) left Puerto Rico for France and painted in the Impressionist style. He became close friends with Paul

JOSÉ FELICIANO

José Feliciano is the most famous Puerto Rican pop musician. He was born in Puerto Rico with congenital glaucoma, which left him blind from birth. When he was 5 years old, his family moved to New York City, where he learned to play the guitar, other string instruments, keyboards, the harmonica, and the trumpet.

Feliciano began working as a singer and musician in the coffee shops of Greenwich Village in his teens, and by 1965 he made his first album, which was a moderate success among Spanish Americans. In 1968 he rose to world fame with the song *Light My Fire*. He performed live at the opening of the fifth game of the 1968 World Series in front of 53,000 spectators in Detroit and millions more worldwide, singing his famous version of *The Star-Spangled Banner*.

Cézanne. One of Oller's paintings hangs in the Louvre in Paris, and many others can be seen in Puerto Rico's museums. *El Velorio*, considered by some to be his best work, shows the mourning of a child's death. Oller paved the way for other painters to use Puerto Rican themes. Miguel Pou and Ramon Frade both painted scenes from Puerto Rican life in the early years of this century.

After World War II, artists such as Lorenzo Homar, J.A. Torres Martinó, and Rafael Tufino founded the Center for Puerto Rican Art in San Juan. Puerto Rican art began to attract foreign collectors and buyers, and more art galleries were opened.

Silkscreen printing was used to produce the first cinema posters and limited editions of some of the best works by Puerto Rican artists. A new generation of artists also experimented with woodcut and linocut techniques. In linocut, the picture is carved into linoleum mounted on a block of wood, then dipped in paint and stamped on paper.

A poster advertising an exhibition on the artistic heritage of the Taino Arawak in Puerto Rico.

Antonio Martorell achieved prominence in the days of pop art, producing playing cards with political cartoons and designing an underground shopping center, the Ondergraun, for teenagers.

In the last 40 years, many Puerto Rican artists, such as Myrna Baez, Ivette Cabrera, and Consuelo Gotay, have studied abroad and incorporated the influence of other parts of the world into their style.

LITERATURE

Folk tales and nature poetry made up Puerto Rico's early literature. But in modern times, social changes have inspired more contemporary literature. Modern writers write about nationality, urban poverty, the loss of innocence as the *jíbaro* become a rarity, and the loss of the old values that held society together.

Early writings that emerged from Puerto Rico are letters and histories written by the early Spanish settlers, or by indigenous men who left the island and wrote about their travels. In 1849 Manuel A. Alonso (1822–89), a medical student from Puerto Rico who lived in Spain, wrote a sociological story about the islanders, describing their daily life in both prose and poetry.

It was not until the 1890s that Puerto Rican islanders began to write novels. Manuel Zeno Gandia (1855–1930) was the first novelist from the island. His most important work, *La Charca* (*The Pond*), published in 1894, symbolizes his view of an island society held back by the church and by feudal landlords.

In the 20th century, René Marqués (1919–79) was the island's most famous writer. He wrote novels, short stories, and plays, and his best-known work is *La Carreta* (*The Oxcart*), a play about a simple farming family moving to New York and struggling to adjust to their new lives.

Enrique Laguerre and modern writers such as Pedro Juan Soto and José Luis Gonzáles have written about the experiences of Puerto Ricans living in the United States. Soto, who lived in New York for 10 years, published his first book, *Spiks*, in 1956. It is a collection of short stories about Puerto Rican families and Puerto Rican society in New York City. Originally written in Spanish and Spanglish, *Spiks* was translated into English in 1973.

Piri Thomas is a writer of Puerto Rican descent born in the United States. He discovered his writing talent while serving a prison sentence for attempted armed robbery. His autobiography, Down These Mean Streets, *is about his life in Spanish Harlem in New York City.*

ARCHITECTURE

Four centuries of Spanish rule have left a legacy of beautiful Spanish colonial architecture in Puerto Rico. Examples are found in San Juan, Ponce, and other early Spanish settlements.

Many parts of San Juan, especially the old walled section built by the Spaniards, still feature Spanish-style architecture and narrow streets cobbled with blue-gray stones once used as ballast on Spanish sailing ships. One aspect of Spanish buildings that fit well with the Taino Arawak settlements was that of a central square, which was important to both cultures. The village squares of the Taino Arawak became plazas under Spanish rule.

An example of Spanish colonial architecture in the Plaza de Armas in San Juan. Many old colonial buildings have been carefully restored by the Institute of Puerto Rican Culture.

LEISURE

PUERTO RICANS TAKE FULL ADVANTAGE of their weekends to relax and unwind. Leisure pursuits on the island range from talking the night away in the town square or listening to outdoor concerts to playing water sports or going to nightclubs.

Elderly Puerto Ricans enjoy playing dominoes or reading books to pass their time, while younger Puerto Ricans, especially in the capital, prefer clubbing or watching movies. Families go on picnics together or visit farms in the countryside. Festivals provide lots of fiesta time.

Spectator sports such as baseball and horse racing are very popular. Gambling in casinos is a major tourist attraction, while gambling at cockfights is a big draw among the locals. Tourists and wealthy Puerto Ricans play golf or engage in water sports and deep-sea fishing, and surfers crowd the beautiful beaches.

Left: **Street concerts are a common sight, with both adults and children taking part.**

Opposite: **A group of Puerto Ricans have fun at a water fountain in San Juan.**

Volleyball players on
Luquillo Beach.

BASEBALL

The national sport of Puerto Rico is baseball, believed to have been introduced by U.S. Marines around the turn of the century. Puerto Rico takes part in the Caribbean League, which is played from October to March, and all the major cities have teams. There are games almost daily in Puerto Rico. Serious fans can watch the Atlanta Braves games on national television, as well as via satellite coverage from the United States.

Many Puerto Ricans have played with the U.S. major leagues. Hiram Bithorn (1916–52) played for the Chicago Cubs, and Luis Olmo (1919–) played for the Brooklyn Dodgers. Orlando Cepeda (1937–) played first base with the San Francisco Giants, then with the Saint Louis Cardinals after recovering from a knee injury. He was voted the National League's most valuable player in 1967. But the greatest Puerto Rican baseball player was Roberto Clemente (1934–72), who spent his entire career with the Pittsburgh Pirates.

Puerto Rico's younger baseball stars include Roberto Alomar, Carlos Delgado, Juan Gonzalez, Ivan Rodriguez, and Bernie Williams.

BOXING

Puerto Rico has produced many successful boxers. Its first boxing champion, Barceloneta native Sixto Escobar (1913–79), won the National Boxing Association bantamweight title three times during the 1930s.

Felix "Tito" Trinidad (1973–), Puerto Rico's reigning boxing world champion, began his career in 1990. He became world welterweight champion in 1993 and world middleweight champion in 2000. After retiring in 2002, he made a triumphant comeback in 2004.

Miguel Cotto (1980–) entered professional boxing in 2001 and won the world light welterweight title in 2004. With his skill and stamina, he has been compared to the legendary "Tito" Trinidad.

ROBERTO CLEMENTE

Roberto Clemente was born in the municipality of Carolina in 1934. He showed his talent in baseball from an early age and played with the island's team, the Santurce Crabbers, while still in school.

When Clemente was 20 years old, talent scouts from the United States came to watch him play. He signed up with the Pittsburgh Pirates in 1955. In his 18 years with the team, he won many awards and honors, including a dozen Gold Glove awards for outstanding fielding.

But it was not just as a baseball player that Puerto Ricans remember Clemente. He was also devoted to his country and came up with the idea of developing a sports city for Puerto Rican children. He gave generously to charities and spent much of his time working for good causes. In 1972, when he was flying to Nicaragua to do relief work at an earthquake site, his plane crashed and he was killed. He was 38.

Clemente was inducted into the Baseball Hall of Fame in 1973 and remains one of the few players ever to hit 3,000 base hits.

COCKFIGHTING

Banned in most parts of the world, cockfighting is a major leisure pursuit in Puerto Rico and a source of income for some. It takes place in *gallera* (gah-YEH-rah), or galleries, all over the island.

The cocks are matched in pairs, and the bird that inflicts the most injuries is the winner. The birds wear spurs and fight

until one dies or flies out of the cockpit. Birds may have pedigrees similar to thoroughbred racehorses and are specially bred for the sport. During a fight, hundreds of dollars change hands in an informal betting system. Few of the profits from gambling are ever declared. This is a sport mainly for working-class men, who supplement their low wages or welfare payments with their winnings.

OTHER SPORTS

Basketball is a popular, largely amateur sport in Puerto Rico. Teams in most of the major cities take part in the Central American and Caribbean Games. While golf is accessible mainly to the wealthy, Puerto Rico's star player, Juan "Chi Chi" Rodriguez (1935–), got acquainted with the sport while working as a caddy. In 1960 he joined the Professional Golf Association tour, and in 1992 he was inducted into the World Golf Hall of Fame.

Horse riding is popular in the northwest of the island at Arenales, on Vieques Island, and at Coamo in the central mountains, where the traditional *paso fino* (pah-soh FEE-noh) horses are bred. Herds of *paso fino* horses also run wild on Vieques Island. An annual *paso fino* show is held in Puerto Rico every year.

Betting at horse races is a major pastime. Puerto Ricans may go to the horse track in San Juan or place their bets at any of hundreds of offtrack betting parlors all over the island.

EVENING PURSUITS

Puerto Ricans like to spend the evening at a street bar or coffee shop, or in the town square, chatting with friends and watching the world go by. People also enjoy playing cards, dominoes, or chess outdoors. On weekends, local *plena* groups perform in the streets. Watching television is also a popular evening leisure activity on the island. Programs are broadcast in Spanish and English, and Puerto Ricans are familiar with most North American and Latin American soap operas.

Gambling at casinos on blackjack tables, roulette wheels, and slot machines, is largely for the wealthy and tourists. Casinos are more formal in Puerto Rico than in the United States, and proper dress is required. A popular form of gambling is the weekly lottery, a big source of revenue for the government. There are also less regulated local lotteries called *la bolita* (lah boh-LEE-tah), which have smaller stakes.

Men playing cards in the street in the cool of the evening.

VACATIONS

Puerto Rico has many unspoiled areas for recreation. Those who prefer to get back to nature can visit the nature reserves or trek through the central mountains. For a short weekend getaway, many families drive into the country for picnics. Alternatively, those who want a break from country life can visit the cities.

Many people take driving holidays around the island, especially city dwellers who go back to the countryside to keep in touch with their rural roots. A popular drive is the 165-mile (265.5-km) Panoramic Route, which follows the Cordillera Central from Yabucoa in the southeast, through forest reserves and rural towns, to Mayagüez on the western coast.

A popular holiday destination for Puerto Rican families is the Coamo spa in the Cordillera Central, which has natural hot springs. The water is a constant 110°F (43°C). Puerto Ricans have all the ingredients for a sunny holiday right at their doorstep. They head southwest to enjoy some of the island's best beaches. Families from San Juan crowd the beach town of Boquerón to escape the hustle and bustle of city life.

Sailing and windsurfing at Ocean Park Beach near San Juan.

ANCIENT BALL GAMES

The Taino Arawak must also have been great sports fans if the remains of their ancient ball courts are anything to go by. Archaeological remains of Taino Arawak ball courts dating back to A.D. 1100 have been found in the Caguana Indian Ceremonial Park near the town of Utuado.

Large rectangular courts were marked out with stones, and remains of what are thought to be belt bats have been found. Belt bats are large stone rings that were worn around the hips and used to hit a ball from one side of the court to another. The teams lost points for letting the ball fall to the ground and gained them for scoring goals.

A 16th-century account of such a game tells of players being carried off the field dead and others wounding their thighs and knees as they hit the ball to the other side of the court. In the ancient Mayan civilization of Mexico, a similar game is depicted on wall friezes. In these, the winning team was allowed to take all the jewelry of the audience, while the losing team was beheaded, so it must have been a very serious game indeed.

FESTIVALS

FESTIVALS AND HOLIDAYS are a year-round affair in Puerto Rico. The island enjoys 20 public holidays, combining some U.S. holidays with its own. There are also patron saint's days, and since each town has a different patron saint, that adds up to a large number of festivals. Many Puerto Rican festivals have street parties with fairgrounds, gambling, and a lot of music.

HOLIDAYS IN PUERTO RICO

January 1	New Year's Day
January 6	Three Kings' Day
January 11	De Hostos' Birthday
January 15	Martin Luther King Jr. Day
January 22	Washington's Birthday
March 22	Emancipation Day
March/April	Good Friday and Easter
April 17	José de Diego's Birthday
May 30	Memorial Day
June 24	San Juan Bautista Day
July 4	Independence Day
July 15	Muñoz Rivera's Birthday
July 25	Constitution Day
July 27	Celsos Barbosa's Birthday
September 1	Labor Day
September 23	Grito de Lares
October 12	Columbus Day
November 11	Veteran's Day
November 19	Discovery of Puerto Rico Day
November	Thanksgiving
December 25	Christmas

Opposite: **A participant dressed up for Carnival in Old San Juan, Puerto Rico.**

PUBLIC HOLIDAYS

Many Puerto Rican holidays commemorate historical events and the birthdays of important citizens.

January 11 is the birthday of Eugenio María de Hostos. He supported the abolition of slavery and independence from Spain. He was exiled from Puerto Rico for his political beliefs and spent several years living in the Dominican Republic.

March 22 commemorates the abolition of slavery in Puerto Rico.

April 17 celebrates the birthday of José de Diego. He was secretary of justice in the few weeks of independence before the Spanish-American War. He became president of the House of Representatives under U.S. rule and spent his political life campaigning for independence.

July 15 is the birthday of Luis Muñoz Rivera. He negotiated autonomy with Spain and later became Puerto Rico's commissioner to the United States.

July 25, Constitution Day, commemorates Puerto Rico's commonwealth status in 1952 and also marks the start of the U.S. invasion of the island.

July 27 marks the birthday of Dr. José Celso Barbosa. He founded the Puerto Rican Republican party in 1857.

September 23 is the anniversary of the first declaration of independence by rebels in Lares. Although the revolt was unsuccessful, it stands out as a time when Puerto Ricans began to fight for their independence. It was made a public holiday in 1968, the centennial of the event.

Children play a big part in Puerto Rico's Grito de Lares celebrations.

November 19, Discovery Day, marks Christopher Columbus' arrival on the island.

LAS NAVIDADES

The most important religious festival in Puerto Rico is Christmas, or Las Navidades, which lasts from around Saint Nicholas Day on December 15 to Three Kings' Day on January 6.

The Christmas season coincides with the start of the tourist season. The island fills with foreign and Puerto Rican visitors. Families have several reunions, starting on Christmas Day.

Thousands of people—even those who hardly go to church—flock to midnight Mass to commemorate the birth of Jesus Christ. The Christmas feast follows with the traditional *léchon asado* (leh-CHON ah-SAH-doh), or roast suckling pig, yucca, chicken, rice, and pigeon peas. Specialty drinks are prepared during this time.

People sing carols and observe the 19th-century tradition of *asaltos* (ah-ZAHL-tohs). Moving in groups from one house to another, they call on friends to join the party. It is a very noisy procession with long stops for welcoming drinks at each house before the party moves on again. The group sings carols, or *villancicos* (vee-yan-SEE-kohs), as it moves around. Children also go around the neighborhood singing carols, beating improvised percussion instruments, and asking for *aguinaldo* (ah-gwee-NAHL-doh), or a small gift.

Easter is also an important religious holiday in Puerto Rico. Every Easter, a statue of the Virgin Mary is carried in a procession around San Juan.

115

A street band entertains passers-by at the Fiesta Calle San Sebastian in San Juan.

The traditional time for gift-giving is Three Kings' Day on January 6, which is a public holiday. On the eve of Three Kings' Day, children fill small boxes with grass for the kings' horses, and their parents replace the grass with gifts for the children. It is also customary for parents to exchange gifts with people with whom they have a *compadrazgo* relationship.

SAINT'S FESTIVALS

While Christmas retains a lot of its religious meaning and is celebrated with formality and reverence, celebrations of patron saint's days usually have the feel of a big party. Street parties, processions, huge dances in the town's central square, traveling fairs, and music are typical of saint's festivals. There are saint's festivals all year round in Puerto Rico, since each town is associated with a particular patron saint.

SAN JUAN BAUTISTA This is the most important saint's day in Puerto Rico. For days before, parties, carnivals, and dances are held in town squares. In the afternoon on June 24, all business activity stops and thousands of families go to the beach, where a party, with salsa music and barbeques, goes on into the night. At midnight, people observe the tradition of walking backward into the sea to greet Saint John the Baptist, the patron saint of Puerto Rico.

NUESTRA SEÑORA DE LA MONSERRATE While most of the saint's festivals in Puerto Rico have taken on the atmosphere of a major party, this one has retained much of its religious tradition. In September each year pilgrims come to the small town of Hormigueros in the island's southwest to celebrate the feast of Our Lady of Monserrat. As a form of penance, they get on their knees and climb the stone stairs of the magnificent Cathedral of Our Lady of Monserrat.

Young people on the steps of a church on Palm Sunday. Some are dressed in clothes from biblical times.

SANTIAGO APOSTOL One of the most famous saint's festivals in Puerto Rico is that of Saint James the Apostle in Loíza. It lasts a week, opening on July 25 with a procession of people in costumes and masks that resemble those still used by the Yoruba in Nigeria.

The festival is of Spanish origin but has many African features. The Christian tradition behind the costumes and masks was to scare lapsed Christians into coming back to church. Carved from coconut shells and painted in bright colors, the masks look like devil's heads with long horns and sharp teeth. It was traditionally the job of the young men who wore the masks to frighten people.

Other participants in Loíza's Santiago Apostol parade include *viejos* (vee-EH-hohs), or old men, masqueraders, and *bomba* dancers, who dance to the beat of the *bomba* drum, an instrument made from a wooden barrel. The dancing is fast and rhythmic, like African dances.

Figures of saints are carried in the processions, and special Masses are celebrated in church. The usual traveling sideshows and fairground rides, small gambling games, and lots of drinking take place alongside the religious element of the festival.

NUESTRA SEÑORA DE GUADALUPE Puerto Rico's second oldest city celebrates a similar saint's festival in February. Like Loíza's festival of Santiago Apostol, the festival of Our Lady of Guadalupe in Ponce also draws on the medieval Christian tradition of using masked men to scare people into repentance.

The African influence is also present in the costumes and music of Ponce's saint's festival, although the masks that its masqueraders wear are made of gourds and have a distinctive style. Processions are held in the city streets near the Cathedral of Our Lady of Guadalupe.

A wall mural shows the Spanish and African traditions of the festival of Santiago Apostol. While a Spanish soldier waves his sword, figures wearing African-style masks and costumes form part of a procession.

CASALS FESTIVAL

Puerto Ricans have celebrated a festival in honor of the famous cellist Pablo Casals, whose mother was Puerto Rican, since he adopted the island as his home in 1957. This festival of classical music has become the greatest cultural and musical event in the Caribbean, with people coming from all over the world to perform.

The Casals Festival takes place in May each year and attracts many famous composers who are happy to have their work premiered in San Juan by the Puerto Rico Symphony Orchestra.

The Pablo Casals Museum in Old San Juan preserves recordings of the Casals Festival as well as Casal's scores and cello.

Sunny Point's Best
SOUTH CAROLINA TOMATOES
GROWN & PACKED BY: SUNNY POINT FARMS WADMALAW ISLAND, SC 29487

FOOD

PUERTO RICAN FOOD combines Spanish, indigenous, and African ingredients and methods. Before the Spaniards came, the islanders' diet included vegetables such as sweet potatoes, cassava, yams, peanuts, corn, and a kind of chili. The Spaniards brought cash crops, vegetables, and meat from all over the Spanish Empire. The cash crops included coffee, coconuts, sugarcane, bananas, and oranges. Potatoes, plantains, and onions supplemented the local vegetables, and those who could afford it added beef, pork, fowl, and goat meat to their diet.

Opposite: **Fresh fruit and vegetables at Plaza Mercado in the Rio Piedras area of San Juan.**

Below: **Bottles of hot chili sauce at a roadside stall.**

These foods were spiced with the arrival of coriander, cumin, ginger, garlic, tomatoes, and newer kinds of chilis. The people of Puerto Rico used these new spices to develop a cooking style that was distinctive—not Taino Arawak, not Spanish, not African, but uniquely Puerto Rican. Although fast foods from the United States are available in Puerto Rico, the ethnic style of cooking is still very popular.

INDIGENOUS FOODS

Puerto Rico's indigenous food staples were corn, cassava, sweet potatoes, yams, peanuts, and some other starchy roots. The Taino Arawak got their supply of meat from birds, iguanas, guinea pigs, oysters, clams, turtles, and other seafood. Their influence is still recognizable in Puerto Rican cooking today.

FOOD

The Taino Arawak made a kind of bread from mashed cassava root mixed with water and baked between two stones. They also made a tea from the flowers of the *campaña* (cahm-PAH-nyah) tree. It had a hallucinogenic effect, and they drank it at religious festivals.

Fresh fruit is plentiful in Puerto Rico, although most of the fruit is unfamiliar to North Americans: hog plum, custard apple (which has a creamy flesh that tastes like custard), genipap, and *quenepa* (keh-NEH-pah), or Spanish lime, which is walnut-sized and has a hard skin that reveals a pink, citrus flesh.

A recreation of how the Taino Arawak cooked. They made cooking and eating utensils from the gourds of the calabash tree.

MEALTIMES

The Spanish tradition of having a long lunch followed by a siesta is not as common in Puerto Rico as might be expected. Eating habits follow individuals' work routines.

In the rural parts of the island, where agriculture is the main activity, people do have long lunches followed by a siesta. But in towns and industrial areas, where lunchtime is a brief break, people eat a light meal and have no time for a siesta. For most people in the city, lunch consists of a sandwich or rice and beans at one of the local *fondas* (FOHN-dahs), or roadside stalls. The evening meal with the family is more elaborate, but this also depends on whether both parents work.

Roadside stalls offer a variety of dishes from which customers can take their pick.

TYPICAL MEALS

Breakfast in Puerto Rican cities is usually boiled or fried eggs with coffee. Breakfast in rural areas is traditionally ground cereal mixed with hot milk.

The mid-day and evening meals include more traditional foods, especially rice and beans, which are the staples of the island. Legumes commonly eaten include white beans, kidney beans, garbanzo beans, and pigeon peas. These are all regular elements of the main meals of the day. The most typical way of cooking beans is in a *sofrito* (soh-FREE-toh) sauce made with bacon or ham, tomatoes, garlic, chili, coriander, and other spices. The beans and sauce are poured over rice and eaten.

Two other important staple foods in Puerto Rico are plantains and bananas. Unripe plantain is sliced and fried to become crisp *tostones* (tohs-TOH-nehs), which are served with rice and *sofrito* sauce, or with meat stews. Ripe yellow plantains and green bananas are boiled and served as vegetables.

Meat is a luxury for poorer families and is not eaten every day. The meat of pigs is made into a variety of dishes, in addition to pork chops and legs of pork. *Mondongo* (mohn-DOHNG-goh) is pig tripe cut in small pieces and stewed in *sofrito* sauce. *Cuchifrito* (cooh-chih-FREE-toh) is stewed pig innards. *Gandinga* (gahn-DING-gah) is stewed pig liver, heart, and kidneys mixed with vegetables. A delicacy called *chicharrón* (chih-chahr-ON) uses large chunks of pig skin as a plate on which meat, rice, and sauce are poured. After eating the meat and rice, people eat the edible plate. But the most famous pork dish, served at traditional Christmas feasts, is *léchon asado*, a young pig that is spit-roasted until the skin is dry and crisp.

Beef is another popular meat in Puerto Rico. Besides a thinly sliced beef steak, there is *carne mechada* (CAR-neh meh-CHAH-dah), a beef roast stuffed with spices and onion. To make a dish called *piononos* (pee-oh-NOH-nohs), ground beef is sautéed in a sauce similar to *sofrito*, sandwiched between fried plantain slices, and then fried again. Another beef dish is cooked *al caldero* (ahl cahl-DEH-roh), that is, in the Puerto Rican cooking pot, a cauldron with a tight-fitting lid.

Chicken is cooked many ways, but one particular specialty is *asopao* (ah-soh-POW), a stew made with chicken and rice.

Fish is less commonly eaten than beef or pork, but one fish staple is salted dried codfish. This is a prime ingredient of a dish served during Lent—*serenata* (zehr-eh-NAH-tah). It is cooked in vinaigrette sauce and served with a salad of tomatoes, avocados, and onions.

Puerto Ricans also have their own snacks. Besides *tostones*, there are meat or codfish fritters, and turnovers called *pastelillos* (pahs-teh-LEE-yohs), which are filled with meat, cheese, or jam.

Many Puerto Rican desserts are based on the locally grown coconut. *Flan de coco* (flan deh COH-coh) is a custard made from coconuts and eggs blended with caramelized sugar. *Bienmesabe* (bee-en-meh-SAH-beh) syrup, made from coconut milk, sugar, and egg yolks, is poured over sponge-cake fingers, ladyfingers, or okra and eaten. A soft cheese made in Puerto Rico is served with fruit as a dessert.

Puerto Rican cooking uses a wide range of spices and herbs.

PUERTO RICAN KITCHENS

In Puerto Rico's capital and other cities, modern kitchens are equipped
with electrical appliances, such as refrigerators and microwave ovens, to
make cooking faster and easier. But in the countryside, things are a little
more in keeping with the old ways of doing things.

The main feature of traditional Puerto Rican kitchens is the *caldero*,
or cauldron, a large, round cast-iron cooking pot, now enhanced with
non-stick features, with a tight-fitting lid. This pot is unique to Puerto
Rico. It is put over a wood-burning stove to cook rice and stews or to
dry-roast meat. The mortar and the pestle are also essential for grinding
fresh seasonings the traditional way.

In homes with a garden, people maintain herb and spice gardens just
outside the door. A selection of herbs, spices, and seasonings identifies

the Puerto Rican kitchen: cloves, ginger, garlic, lime rind, and coriander, among others. Most ingredients are bought fresh from the market; fruit and vegetables are easily available from local farms, as is a soft, white cow's milk cheese. Supermarkets sell processed food products from the United States, but these tend to be expensive and are rare in traditional Puerto Rican kitchens.

PUERTO RICO'S CULINARY FUTURE

Factors affecting the future of food in Puerto Rico include safety and innovation. The safety of Puerto Ricans' food supply rests on their farming and food-processing methods and on environmental conditions on and around the island. Innovation has taken Puerto Rico's traditional cuisine beyond the traditional Puerto Rican kitchen and introduced the island's tasty treasures to a wider audience.

SAFETY Within the framework of U.S. federal laws, Puerto Rico's departments of agriculture and health administer programs prohibiting the adulteration of food products manufactured or sold on the island. These authorities ensure compliance with food regulations by conducting inspections of food products and imposing penalties on violators.

Environmental damage can contaminate farm harvests and harm consumers' health. For example, studies point to the possibility that fish containing high levels of toxic chemicals in the waters around Vieques could pose a health risk to the islanders who consume the fish.

Food biotechnology is of special concern to Puerto Rico, which is one of the United States' test fields for genetically modified crops. Activists around the world have been campaigning for laws requiring manufacturers to label food products that are genetically modified.

AUTHENTICITY AND INNOVATION While some Puerto Rican chefs are using traditional recipes to preserve the authenticity of home-style Puerto Rican cooking in restaurants, others have taken their country's cuisine to new heights in innovative ways, by experimenting with fusion—combining Puerto Rican ingredients or cooking styles with those of other cultures.

The famous Piña Colada cocktail is made from rum.

RUM

The development of the sugar industry resulted in the production of rum, one of Puerto Rico's more important products. The island is one of the top rum producers in the world and supplies around 75 percent of rums in the United States.

Molasses, a byproduct of sugar, is used to make rum. When molasses comes into contact with yeast, it begins to ferment and reacts with the yeast to produce alcohol. In the early years of Spanish rule, this process was used to make a wine called *aguardiente* (ah-goo-are-dee-EN-teh), which was widely drunk. To make rum, the wine is distilled to evaporate most of the water content and remove impurities.

Today rum is made in computerized plants with carefully controlled yeast strains added to the molasses. This mixture ferments in large stainless steel vats to produce the wine, which is then put into a huge still to drive off the excess water. The alcohol obtained is very strong.

Variations in storage and treatment create silver or gold rum. Silver (white) rum is filtered to remove the taste of the molasses; the result is a clear, light, and dry alcohol, which is usually mixed in cocktails. Gold (amber) rum goes through a longer aging process and contains more molasses. It has a strong flavor and a deep color and is usually drunk plain. Puerto Rico is known more for its white rums; Bacardi is its most famous brand.

COFFEE

Coffee has diminished in importance in the past decades because the costs of production have risen so much. But it is still grown on the lower slopes of some mountains where the good drainage suits the plants. Whether it is due to the plant variety, the climate, or the treatment of the plant, Puerto Rican coffee is stronger than typical North American coffee. In the late 19th century, Puerto Rican coffee, called Yauco after the place where it was grown, was considered one of the world's best.

During the day coffee is drunk *con leche* (con LEH-cheh), with a half portion of milk and a half portion of very strong coffee. After dinner it is drunk demitasse, in a tiny cup and black with sugar. Coffee is served in tiny paper cups all over the island at small roadside stalls, more as a stimulant than as a thirst quencher.

An ice-cream vendor in old San Juan.

ESCABECHE DE GUINEOS

This sumptuous dish of pickled green bananas and chicken gizzards may be eaten with rice, with other dishes, or on its own. This recipe serves six.

5 pounds (2 kg) green bananas
2 pounds (900 g) chicken gizzards
1 bulb garlic
$\frac{1}{2}$ cup olive oil
Salt and pepper to taste
2 large Spanish onions, thinly sliced
$\frac{1}{2}$ pound (230 g) black olives

Boil the bananas for 20 minutes. Drain, and set aside. Boil the chicken gizzards for 2 hours until very tender. Drain, cut into small pieces, and set aside. Puree the garlic. Mix with the olive oil, salt, and pepper. Slice the bananas half-inch (1-cm) thick. Mix well with the chicken gizzards, garlic, olive oil, onions, and olives. Bake for 20 to 30 minutes at 325°F (162.8°C). Serve hot.

SURULLITOS

These cheese and cornmeal sticks are a popular Puerto Rican snack. They are best eaten hot with spicy stews or as a bread.

1 $^1/_2$ cups water
1 teaspoon salt
$^3/_4$ cup yellow cornmeal
$^1/_2$ cup grated cheddar cheese
A little vegetable oil for frying

Boil the water in a saucepan, and add salt. Add the cornmeal, pouring steadily and stirring constantly to prevent lumps from forming. Cook for 5 minutes over a low fire until the mixture is thick and smooth. Turn off the heat, and add the cheese. Leave to cool. Heat the oil in a large frying pan. Shape the cheese and cornmeal mixture into sticks 3 inches (7.5 cm) long and 1 inch (2.5 cm) thick. Fry the sticks two at a time until evenly browned. Serve hot.

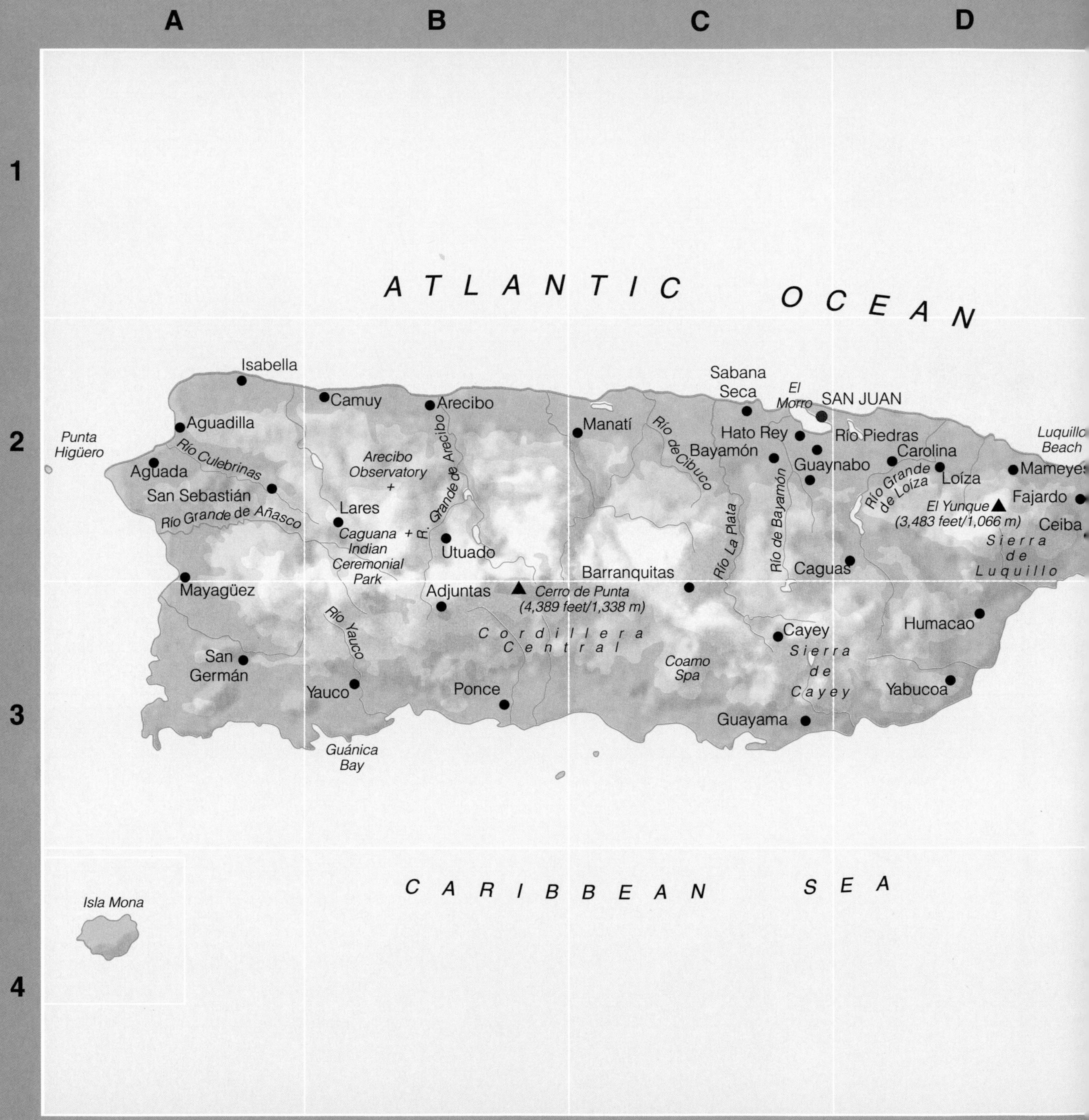

A   B   C   D

1

2

3

4

ATLANTIC OCEAN

CARIBBEAN SEA

Punta Higüero

Isabella

Camuy

Aguadilla

Aguada

Río Culebrinas

San Sebastián

Río Grande de Añasco

Mayagüez

San Germán

Yauco

Río Yauco

Guánica Bay

Arecibo

Arecibo Observatory

Lares

Caguana Indian Ceremonial Park

R. Grande de Arecibo

Utuado

Adjuntas

Cerro de Punta (4,389 feet/1,338 m)

Cordillera Central

Ponce

Manatí

Río de Cibuco

Barranquitas

Río La Plata

Coamo Spa

Guayama

Sabana Seca

El Morro

SAN JUAN

Hato Rey

Bayamón

Guaynabo

Río de Bayamón

Caguas

Cayey

Sierra de Cayey

Río Piedras

Carolina

Loíza

Río Grande de Loíza

El Yunque (3,483 feet/1,066 m)

Luquillo Beach

Mameyes

Fajardo

Ceiba

Sierra de Luquillo

Humacao

Yabucoa

Isla Mona

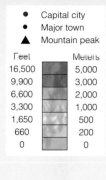

E

- ● Capital city
- ● Major town
- ▲ Mountain peak

Feet		Meters
16,500		5,000
9,900		3,000
6,600		2,000
3,300		1,000
1,650		500
660		200
0		0

Culebra

Vieques

N

MAP OF PUERTO RICO

Adjuntas, B3
Aguada, A2
Aguadilla, A2
Arecibo, B2
Arecibo Observatory, B2
Atlantic Ocean, A1–E1, A2–E2

Barceloneta, B2
Barranquitas, C3
Bayamón, C2

Caguana Indian Ceremonial Park, B2
Caguas, D2
Camuy, B2
Caribbean Sea, A3–E3, A4–E4
Carolina, D2
Cayey, C3
Ceiba, D2
Cerro de Punta, B3
Coamo Spa, C3
Cordillera Central, B3–C3
Culebra, E2

El Morro, C2
El Yunque, D2

Fajardo, D2

Guánica Bay, B3

Guayama, C3
Guaynabo, C2

Isabella, A2

Hato Rey, C2
Humacao, D3

Lares, B2
Loíza, D2
Luquillo Beach, D2

Mameyes, D2
Manati, C2
Mayagüez, A2
Mona, A4

Ponce, B3
Punta Higüero, A2

Río Culebrinas, A2
Río de Bayamón, C2
Río de Cibuco, C2

Río Grande de Añasco, A2
Río Grande de Arecibo, B2
Río Grande de Loíza, D2
Río La Plata, C2
Río Piedras, C2
Río Yauco, B3

Sabana Seca, C2
San Germán, A3
San Juan, C2
San Sebastián, A2
Sierra de Cayey, C3–D3
Sierra de Luquillo, D2

Utuado, B2

Vieques, E3

Yabucoa, D3
Yauco, B3

ECONOMIC PUERTO RICO

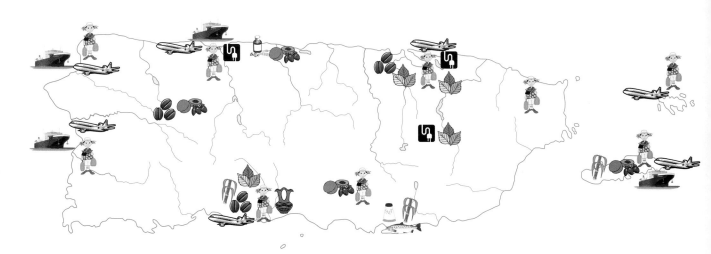

Manufacturing

 Electrical Appliances

Handicrafts

Pharmaceuticals

Agriculture

Coffee

Fruit

Sugarcane

Tobacco

Services

 Airport

Port

Tourism

Natural Resources

Fish

Salt

ABOUT THE ECONOMY

OVERVIEW
From the mid-1940s, Operation Bootstrap played a key role in transforming Puerto Rico from a largely agricultural to a full-fledged industrial economy. In 1996 the cessation of the island's special tax-break status under Section 936 led to a decline in U.S. investments. Puerto Rico has rejuvenated its economy through its flourishing tourism sector.

GROSS DOMESTIC PRODUCT (GDP)
$65.21 billion (2004 estimate)

GDP BY SECTOR
Agriculture 1 percent, industry 45 percent, services 54 percent (2002 estimate)

AGRICULTURAL PRODUCTS
Sugarcane, coffee, plantains, fruit, tobacco, livestock

INDUSTRIAL PRODUCTS
Pharmaceuticals, electronics, clothing, food products

INFLATION RATE
6.5 percent (2003 estimate)

CURRENCY
1 U.S. dollar (USD) = 100 cents

WORKFORCE
1.3 million (2000)

WORKFORCE BY OCCUPATION
Agriculture 3 percent, industry 20 percent, services 77 percent (2000 estimate)

UNEMPLOYMENT RATE
12 percent (2002)

TRADE PARTNERS
United States, Ireland, Japan, United Kingdom, Netherlands, Dominican Republic

EXPORTS
Chemicals, natural gas, electronics, medical equipment, clothing, food products

IMPORTS
Chemicals, petroleum products, natural gas, machinery and equipment, clothing, food products

PORTS
Aguadilla, Arecibo, Guayama, Mayagüez, Ponce, San Juan, Vieques

AIRPORTS
Culebra, Isla Grande (San Juan), Domingo Ruiz (Arecibo), Eugenio María de Hostos (Mayagüez), Luis Muñoz Marín International (Carolina), Mercedita (Ponce), Rafael Hernandez (Aguadilla), Vieques

CULTURAL PUERTO RICO

Juan A. Rivero Zoo
The island's only zoo is in Mayaguez, the third largest city in Puerto Rico. The zoo is home to a variety of mammals, birds, and reptiles.

Arecibo Observatory
Part of the National Astronomy and Ionosphere Center, the observatory at Arecibo has one of the world's most powerful radar-radio telescopes, which provides scientists around the world with data for research in astronomy and planetary and atmospheric studies.

Old San Juan
The capital city's 465-year-old neighborhood consists of carefully restored 16th- and 17th-century Spanish colonial buildings, including the El Morro Fort and the San Juan Cathedral.

Fiestas Patronales
This nine-day festival in Loiza features salsa dancing and masquerading. Populated largely by the descendents of the Yoruba from Nigeria, Loiza presents a uniquely different culture than most Puerto Rican cities.

Caguana Indian Ceremonial Park
This park, surrounded by limestone terrain, preserves monoliths dating back to the earliest Taíno Arawak civilization on the island.

Old Ponce
Recently given a facelift costing nearly half a billion dollars, the island's second-largest city preserves the glory of its colonial-era churches, houses, plazas, and fountains.

El Yunque
This mountain in the Sierra de Luquillo is part of a forest reserve by the same name. Set aside by the Spaniards in 1876, this protected area preserves some of the oldest virgin forest in the region.

Mosquito Bay
Millions of luminescent microscopic marine creatures light up at the slightest movement in the Mosquito Bay on Vieques, a former U.S. Navy training ground. Vieques also houses the last Spanish fort, now a museum.

ABOUT THE CULTURE

COUNTRY NAME
Commonwealth of Puerto Rico

CAPITAL
San Juan

OTHER MAJOR CITIES
Aguadilla, Arecibo, Bayamón, Fajardo, Caguas, Carolina, Cayey, Guaynabo, Mayagüez, Ponce

NATIONAL FLAG
Five horizontal bands (red and white); a blue isosceles triangle based on the hoist side, with a white five-point star in the center

POPULATION
3.9 million (2005 estimate)

LIFE EXPECTANCY
78 years; men 74 years, women 82 years (2005 estimate)

AGE STRUCTURE
0–14 years: 22 percent; 15–64 years: 65.5 percent; 65 years and above: 12.5 percent (2005 estimate)

ETHNIC GROUPS
White 80.5 percent, black 8 percent, other 11.5 percent

RELIGIOUS GROUPS
Roman Catholic 85 percent, Protestant and other 15 percent

LANGUAGES
Spanish and English

LITERACY RATE
94.1 percent (2002)

IMPORTANT ANNIVERSARIES
Three Kings Day (January 6), Emancipation Day (March 11), Muñoz Rivera's Birthday (July 17), Constitution Day (July 25), Grito de Lares Day (September 23), Discovery of Puerto Rico Day (November 19)

LEADERS IN POLITICS
Luis Muñoz Rivera (1859–1916)—statesman who worked for Puerto Rican autonomy; resident commissioner in the United States (1910–16)
Luis Muñoz Marín—Puerto Rico's first elected governor (1948–64)
Sila María Calderón—Puerto Rico's first female governor (2001–04)

LEADERS IN THE ARTS
Pablo Casals and Tito Puente (music), Manuel Zeno Gandia and René Marqués (literature), José Campeche and Francisco Oller y Cestero (painting)

LEADERS IN SPORTS
Roberto Clemente (baseball), Juan "Chi Chi" Rodriguez (golf), Felix "Tito" Trinidad (boxing)

TIME LINE

IN PUERTO RICO	IN THE WORLD
	753 B.C. Rome is founded.
200 B.C. Igneri arrive from Venezuela.	**116–17 B.C.** The Roman Empire reaches its greatest extent, under Emperor Trajan (98–17).
	A.D. 600 Height of Mayan civilization
A.D. 1000 Taino Arawak populate the island.	**1000** The Chinese perfect gunpowder and begin to use it in warfare.
1493 Christopher Columbus reaches Puerto Rico.	
1508 First Spanish settlement in Puerto Rico	
1511 The Taino Arawak rebel for the first time against the Spaniards.	
1519 The government center moves to San Juan.	
1528 French privateers attack Puerto Rico, destroying many settlements.	**1530** Beginning of transatlantic slave trade organized by the Portuguese in Africa.
1599 British forces capture San Juan but are soon repelled.	**1558–1603** Reign of Elizabeth I of England
1625 Dutch forces burn San Juan to the ground.	**1620** Pilgrims sail the *Mayflower* to America.
	1776 U.S. Declaration of Independence
	1789–99 The French Revolution
	1861 The U.S. Civil War begins.
1868 Puerto Ricans rebel against the Spaniards.	**1869** The Suez Canal is opened.
1873 Slavery is abolished in Puerto Rico.	

IN PUERTO RICO	IN THE WORLD
1898	
Led by Luis Muñoz Rivera, Puerto Rico gains autonomy from Spain, but the Treaty of Paris transfers the island to the United States.	**1914** World War I begins.
1917 Jones Act offers Puerto Ricans U.S. citizenship.	
1941 The U.S. Navy sets up military bases on the islands of Vieques and Culebra.	**1939** World War II begins. **1945** The United States drops atomic bombs on Hiroshima and Nagasaki.
1948 Luis Muñoz Marín becomes Puerto Rico's first elected governor.	**1949** The North Atlantic Treaty Organization (NATO) is formed.
1952 The island is proclaimed the Commonwealth of Puerto Rico.	**1957** The Russians launch Sputnik.
1967 Puerto Ricans overwhelmingly vote to maintain their commonwealth status.	**1966–69** The Chinese Cultural Revolution
1976 Section 936 gives special tax breaks to U.S. companies doing business in Puerto Rico.	**1986** Nuclear power disaster at Chernobyl in Ukraine
1991 Spanish is declared the only official language of Puerto Rico.	**1991** Break-up of the Soviet Union
1993 English is officiated as the national language alongside Spanish.	
1996 Section 936 is repealed.	**1997** Hong Kong is returned to China.
2001 Síla María Calderon is elected the first female governor of the island.	**2001** Terrorists crash planes in New York, Washington, D.C., and Pennsylvania.
2004 Anibal Acevedo-Vila is elected governor.	**2003** War in Iraq

GLOSSARY

barrio
The local area or neighborhood.

batey (BAH-teh)
The central square of a Taino Arawak village.

caldero (cahl-DEH-roh)
A traditional large, round cooking pot with a tight lid.

compadrazgo (cohm-pahd-RAZ-goh)
The relationship between close friends, similar to that between godparents.

compadre (cohm-PAH-dreh)
A godfather, usually a close family friend.

coquí (koh-KEE)
A small tree frog.

décima (DEH-see-mah)
An improvised poetic form consisting of 10 eight-syllabic verses.

güiro (GWEE-roh)
A traditional percussion instrument made and played by the Taino Arawak.

jíbaro (HEE-bah-row)
A peasant farmer.

jurakan (hoo-rah-KAHN)
Taino Arawak word meaning devil, from which the English word hurricane is derived.

karst
A landscape of sinkholes and underground tunnels formed by erosion in limestone rock.

paso fino (pah-soh FEE-noh)
A traditional breed of horse.

pastelillos (pahs-teh-LEE-yohs)
Turnovers filled with meat, cheese, or jam.

patrón (pah-TRON)
Local landowner in rural areas.

sofrito (soh-FREE-toh)
A basic sauce made with bacon or ham, tomatoes, garlic, chili, coriander, and other spices.

Taino Arawak
The indigenous people who inhabited Puerto Rico before the Spanish arrival.

tostones (tohs-TOH-nehs)
Unripe plantains sliced and fried until crisp.

trigueño (trih-GEN-yoh)
Puerto Rico's mixed-ancestry majority.

vejigante (veh-GAHN-teh)
Masks made to scare people into repentance; they later became symbols of anticolonialism.

yuca (YOO-kah)
Cassava. A traditional food of the Taino Arawak and a common ingredient in Puerto Rican food.

FURTHER INFORMATION

BOOKS

Delano, Jack (photographer). *Puerto Rico Mio: Four Decades of Change*. Washington, D.C.: Smithsonian Institution Press, 1990.

Hernández, Carmen Dolores. *Puerto Rican Voices in English: Interviews With Writers*. Westport, CT: Praeger Publishers, 1997.

Muckley, Robert L. and Adela Martínez-Santiago. *Stories from Puerto Rico / Historias de Puerto Rico*. Side By Side Bilingual Books Series. Lincolnwood, IL: Passport Books, 1999.

Ortiz, Yvonne. *A Taste of Puerto Rico: Traditional and New Dishes from the Puerto Rican Community*. New York: Plume, 1997.

Santiago, Esmeralda. *When I Was Puerto Rican*. New York: Vintage Books, 1994.

WEBSITES

About Puerto Rico (more than 200 web pages about the island). www.dollarman.com/puertorico

BBC News Country Profiles: Regions and Territories: Puerto Rico.
http://news.bbc.co.uk/2/hi/americas/country_profiles/3593469.stm

Central Intelligence Agency World Factbook (select Puerto Rico in the country list).
www.cia.gov/cia/publications/factbook

Pharmaceutical Industry Association of Puerto Rico. www.piapr.com

Puerto Rico Herald. www.puertorico-herald.org

Puerto Rico Industrial Development Company of the Commonwealth of Puerto Rico (PRIDCO).
www.pridco.com

Puerto Rico Manufacturers Association. www.prma.com

Puerto Rico Tourism Company. www.gotopuertorico.com

U.S. Environmental Protection Agency (type "Puerto Rico" or "Region 2" in the search box).
www.epa.gov

Welcome to Puerto Rico. http://welcome.topuertorico.org

MUSIC

Jíbaro Hasta el Hueso: Mountain Music of Puerto Rico by Ecos de Borinquen. Smithsonian Folkways Recordings, 2003.

Puerto Rico. Putumayo Presents Series. Putumayo World Music, 2000.

VIDEO

Boricua Béisbol: The Passion of Puerto Rico. Major League Baseball Productions. WEA, 2003.

The Sights and Sounds of Puerto Rico. Hispanic Culture Series. Video Knowledge, 2004.

BIBLIOGRAPHY

Aliotta, Jerome J. *The Puerto Ricans*. Peoples of North America Series. New York: Chelsea House Publishers, 1991.

Hauberg, Clifford A. *Puerto Rico and the Puerto Ricans*. Immigrant Heritage of America Series. New York: Twayne Publishers, 1974.

Jiménez de Wagenheim, Olga. *Puerto Rico's Revolt for Independence: El Grito de Lares*. Boulder, CO: Westview Press, 1985.

Morales Carrión, Arturo. *Puerto Rico: A Political and Cultural History*. New York: WW Norton & Company, 1983.

Pariser, Harry S. *Adventure Guide to Puerto Rico*. Edison, NJ: Hunter Publishing, 1989.

Porter, Darwin and Danforth Prince. *Frommer's Puerto Rico: Including Vieques & Culebra* (7th edition). New York: Wiley Publishing, Inc., 2004.

Rodriguez, Clara E. *Puerto Ricans: Born in the USA*. Boston, MA: Unwin Hyman, 1989.

Wagenheim, Kal. *Puerto Rico: A Profile*. New York: Praeger Publishers, 1970.

Insight Guide: Puerto Rico. Hong Kong: APA Publications, 1987.

CIA World Factbook: Puerto Rico. www.cia.gov/cia/publications/factbook/geos/rq.html

Government of Puerto Rico. http://en.wikipedia.org/wiki/Government_of_Puerto_Rico

Leisure Activities in Puerto Rico. www.zonalatina.com/Zldata94.htm

National Astronomy and Ionosphere Center: Arecibo Observatory. www.naic.edu/public/the_telescope.htm

Pharmaceutical Industry Association of Puerto Rico. www.piapr.com

Puerto Rico Industrial Development Company of the Commonwealth of Puerto Rico (PRIDCO). www.pridco.com

Puerto Rico Manufacturers Association. www.prma.com

Santeria Religion in Puerto Rico. http://saxakali.com/caribbean/dviteri.htm

U.S. Environmental Protection Agency. www.epa.gov

Welcome to Puerto Rico. http://welcome.topuertorico.org

INDEX